DSA
DRIVING STANDARDS AGENCY
SAFE RIDING FOR LIFE™

The **OFFICIAL DSA GUIDE** to
RIDING
the essential skills

Approved by
Plain
English
Campaign

London: TSO

Written and compiled by the Learning Materials Section of the Driving Standards Agency (DSA).

Published with the permission of the Driving Standards Agency on behalf of the Controller of Her Majesty's Stationery Office.

Previously known as *Motorcycle Riding - the essential skills*
First edition 1991
Second edition 1996
Third edition 1999
Fourth edition 2001

New title - *The Official DSA Guide to Riding - the essential skills*
First edition 2005
Third impression 2008

ISBN 978 011552644 2

A CIP catalogue record for this book is available from the British Library.

Other titles in the official DSA series

The Official DSA Theory Test for Car Drivers
The Official DSA Theory Test for Motorcyclists
The Official DSA Theory Test for Drivers of Large Vehicles
The Official DSA Guide to Learning to Drive
Helping Learners to Practise - the official DSA guide
The Official DSA Guide to Driving - the essential skills
The Official DSA Guide to Learning to Ride
The Official DSA Guide to Driving Buses and Coaches
The Official DSA Guide to Driving Goods Vehicles
The Official DSA Guide to Tractor and Specialist Vehicle Driving Tests
The Official DSA Theory Test for Car Drivers (CD-Rom)
The Official DSA Theory Test for Motorcyclists (CD-Rom)
The Official DSA Theory Test for Drivers of Large Vehicles (CD-Rom)
The Official DSA Guide to Hazard Perception (DVD) (also available on VHS)
Prepare for your Practical Driving Test (DVD)

Acknowledgements

The Driving Standards Agency would like to thank their staff and the Department for Transport for their contribution to the production of this publication.

75% recycled
This book is printed
on 75% recycled paper

Directgov

Directgov is the place to find all government motoring information and services. From logbooks to licensing, from driving tests to road tax, go to:

www.direct.gov.uk/motoring

Theory and practical tests
www.direct.gov.uk/drivingtest

Theory & Practical Tests
Enquiries & Bookings **0300 200 1122**
Welsh speakers **0300 200 1133**

Practical Tests
Minicom **0300 200 1144**
Fax **0300 200 1155**

Theory Tests
Minicom **0300 200 1166**
Fax **0300 200 1177**
Customer Enquiry Unit **0300 200 1188**

Driving Standards Agency
www.dsa.gov.uk

Stanley House, 56 Talbot Street, Nottingham NG1 5GU

Tel **0115 901 2500**
Fax **0115 901 2510**

(from March 2008: The Axis Building, 112 Upper Parliament Street, Nottingham NG1 6LP
Tel 0115 936 6666)

Driver & Vehicle Licensing Agency
www.dvla.gov.uk

Longview Road, Swansea SA6 7JL

Tel **0870 240 0009**
Fax **01792 783 071**
Minicom **01792 782 787**

DVA (Northern Ireland)

Theory test **0845 600 6700**
Practical test **0870 247 2471**

Driver & Vehicle Agency (Testing) in Northern Ireland
www.dvani.gov.uk

Balmoral Road, Belfast BT12 6QL

Tel **02890 681 831**
Fax **02890 665 520**

Driver & Vehicle Agency (Licensing) in Northern Ireland
www.dvani.gov.uk

County Hall, Castlerock Road, Coleraine BT51 3TB

Tel **02870 341 469**
24 hour tel **0345 111 222**
Minicom **02870 341 380**

Office of the Parliamentary Commissioner for Administration
(The Parliamentary Ombudsman)

Millbank Tower, Millbank, London SW1P 4QP

Tel **020 7217 4163**
Fax **020 7217 4160**

The National Association for Bikers with a Disability
www.nabd.org.uk

Unit 20, The Bridgewater Centre, Urmston Manchester M41 7TE

Tel **0844 415 4849**

The Disabled Motorcyclists Association
www.thedma.org.uk

Ada House, 77 Thompson Street Manchester M4 5FY

Tel **0161 833 8817**

The Driving Standards Agency (DSA) is an executive agency of the Department for Transport. You'll see its logo at theory and practical test centres.

DSA aims to promote road safety through the advancement of driving standards, by

- establishing and developing high standards and best practice in driving and riding on the road; before people start to drive, as they learn, and after they pass their test
- ensuring high standards of instruction for different types of driver and rider
- conducting the statutory theory and practical tests efficiently, fairly and consistently across the country
- providing a centre of excellence for driver training and driving standards
- developing a range of publications and other publicity material designed to promote safe driving for life.

The Driving Standards Agency recognises and values its customers. We will treat all our customers with respect, and deliver our services in an objective, polite and fair way.

www.dsa.gov.uk

The Driver and Vehicle Agency (DVA) is an executive agency within the Department of the Environment for Northern Ireland.

Its primary aim is to promote and improve road safety through the advancement of driving and riding standards and implementation of the Government's policies for improving the mechanical standards of vehicles.

www.dvani.gov.uk

Contents

section **one**
THE RIDER

This section covers
- Your attitude
- New riders
- Returning riders
- Budgeting

A message from the Chief Driving Examiner

Motorcycling can be a pleasant and exhilarating experience, as well as an economic means of transport. However, the volume of traffic and faster, more powerful motorcycles make it essential, more than ever before, for riders to be ready to deal with the unexpected and question the actions of other road users. After all, it's in your interest to make safety your responsibility.

Whether you're an experienced motorcyclist or a new rider you'll realise that riding not only requires skill in handling your machine but also the ability to 'read' the road. Good observation and anticipation are essential to safe riding.

This book is a step-by-step guide to motorcycling, covering all aspects: from choosing your machine and the correct protective clothing to defensive riding and the importance of proper training. It's an essential reference book for all motorcyclists, however experienced - instructors too. Read it carefully and put into practice the advice it gives.

Above all, make sure that your aim is 'Safe riding for life'.

Trevor Wedge

Driving Standards Agency
Chief Driving Examiner and Director of Safer Driving

Your attitude

Riding a motorcycle can be great fun and is enjoyed by people of all ages. However, riding on the road means accepting responsibility for yourself and showing due care and consideration for all other road users.

Compared with driving other vehicles, riding a motorcycle puts you at greater risk from other road users. If you're involved in an accident the chances of being injured are very high.

Be considerate in queuing traffic. You should avoid obstructing junctions so that the way is clear for turning traffic

The machine, the special clothing, the road, the weather, and the traffic are all part of the environment of motorcycling. How well you get on depends on you.

This section covers the attitude and approach you need to ensure that you enjoy a long and safe motorcycling career.

A good rider isn't a perfect rider; it's very doubtful if such a rider exists. A good rider always tries to set a good example by showing

- responsibility
- anticipation
- patience
- concentration
- expertise.

Together, these qualities go to make up what is generally known as the rider's attitude. The importance of attitude to safe riding cannot be stressed enough. The attitude you take to motorcycling will influence the type of rider you become.

Take pride in your riding and you'll develop a positive attitude. This won't always be easy, but keep working at it.

It's a fact that nearly all road accidents are caused by human error. Reducing that risk is the responsibility of us all.

When you ride on the road other people's safety depends on your responsible behaviour

Allowing space can help you anticipate and respond safely to other people's actions

Responsibility

To be a responsible rider you should always be concerned for the safety of all road users.

This includes

- yourself and your passenger
- other drivers and riders
- cyclists
- pedestrians, particularly the most vulnerable such as children, the elderly and people with disabilities.

Be responsible by recognising your own limitations. Riding beyond the bounds of caution is foolish and irresponsible.

Develop the right attitude from the beginning and you'll become a safe and responsible rider.

Anticipation

When you're riding a motorcycle it's vital that you plan ahead. This means acting before situations get out of control. As a motorcyclist you have to consider

- other road users. They don't always do what you expect. Question their actions and be ready for the unexpected
- the road. How sharp is the next bend? What's around the next corner? Can you stop within your range of vision? Road signs and road markings are there to help you plan ahead
- the conditions. You'll be exposed to the weather and affected by the road conditions. Slippery surfaces are especially dangerous for motorcyclists.

The volume of traffic on today's roads inevitably leads to congestion and delays. Showing patience and restraint will help keep you safe and sets a good example

Patience

Try not to over-react if another road user does something wrong. Control your desire to retaliate. Everyone can make a mistake, including you. You should make allowances for other people's mistakes just as you'd want them to make allowances for yours.

Showing good manners is the hallmark of a skillful rider. Others will learn from watching you and will appreciate your courtesy and good riding.

Traffic jams and delays can cause frustration. Avoid the need to rush. Set out with plenty of time to spare. It's always better to arrive late than not at all.

Concentration

Riding on today's roads demands full concentration. If you're driving a car, a lapse in concentration may only dent your pride (and your car). Motorcycles aren't so forgiving. Your survival will depend on your concentration.

Many factors can disrupt your concentration such as

- fatigue
- your health
- being cold or wet
- worries
- alcohol or drugs
- mobile phones.

It's in your own interest not to ride if you know you can't concentrate fully.

Fatigue - Tiredness can creep up on anyone and may go unnoticed until it is too late. Boredom or monotony can increase the likelihood of fatigue such as when riding

- at night
- in fog
- on motorways.

The likelihood of suffering from fatigue may be further increased by

- chilling effects of the weather
- noise and vibration.

Don't start a journey if you're already feeling tired. If you feel tired while riding stop at a safe place and rest until you feel you can continue safely. On a motorway rest at the nearest service area or leave the motorway. Do not pull up on the hard shoulder just to rest.

When you plan your journey remember to include time for breaks and refreshment.

Your health - If you're feeling ill, this can upset your concentration. A bad cold can distract your mind and slow your reactions. If you feel tired or unwell don't ride.

Being cold and wet - Without proper clothing you can get very cold and wet when riding a motorcycle. Hands and feet are especially susceptible. Being cold and wet will reduce your ability to concentrate and slow your reactions.

Worries - If something upsets or worries you think twice before starting a journey. If you can't concentrate on your riding consider using some other means of transport.

Wearing ear plugs helps to reduce fatigue caused by noise and prevent hearing damage

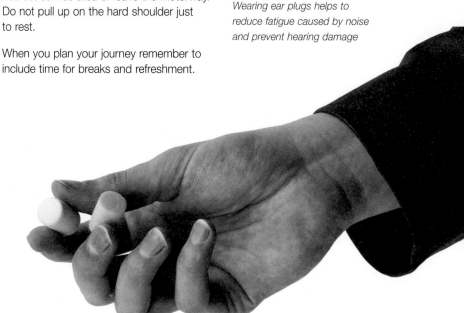

Alcohol - This will reduce your ability to ride safely. The law sets the limit of 80 milligrams of alcohol per 100 millilitres of blood. It's an offence to ride a motorcycle or a moped if you exceed this level.

If you drink in the evening you may still be over the limit and unfit to ride the following morning.

If you want to be safe and you're going to ride don't drink at all.

Drugs - Taking certain drugs is a criminal offence. Riding when you're under their influence can seriously impair your concentration, and the outcome could be fatal.

> **Remember,** riding under the influence of alcohol or drugs could invalidate your insurance.

If your doctor prescribes medicines for you, ask if they'll affect your ability to ride safely. Some over-the-counter medicines can also affect you. Read the label. If in doubt ask the chemist or your doctor.

The responsibility is yours.

Mobile phones - You must not use a hand-held mobile phone, or other similar device when riding, except to call 999 or 112 in a genuine emergency.

Find a safe place to stop before making a call. Use voicemail to receive calls and make regular stops to retrieve messages

Using any phone or microphone, even if it is hands-free, can distract your attention from the road. It is safer not to use any phone while riding.

Riding requires all of your attention all of the time.

Expertise

Master the techniques set out in this manual. They were developed by experienced riders and they make sense.

Develop safe habits and a responsible attitude from the very beginning. Always think about how other road users will be affected by your actions.

Think 'safety'.

New riders

Young and inexperienced motorcyclists are more vulnerable on the roads. They can often be involved in accidents early in their motorcycling careers, sometimes tragically so. Such accidents can usually be attributed to

- the natural exuberance of youth
- immaturity; an inability to cope with the serious nature of riding a motorcycle
- showing off
- competitive behaviour, racing and so on
- lack of experience and judgement
- being over-confident of their own ability.

Things to avoid

- riding too fast; speed can kill
- riding without consideration and care
- showing off; if you want to impress your friends, show them how safe a rider you are
- being 'wound up'; keep calm, learn to ignore the stupidity of others
- an aggressive attitude and behaviour
- riding beyond your capabilities; always leave yourself a safety margin
- being distracted.

Above all, be responsible and always show courtesy and consideration to other road users. Your life, and the lives of others, could depend on it.

Be safe, don't take risks!

False perceptions

Many young and inexperienced motorcyclists wrongly believe that the ability to handle their motorcycle will make them a good and safe rider. They fail to recognise that handling skill alone will not prevent accidents.

Having the right attitude of mind and a sound knowledge of defensive riding techniques is essential.

Returning riders

If you return to motorcycling after an absence of several years you'll probably find a lot has changed. This will include

- road and traffic conditions
- motorcycle technology
- your skills.

While you may continue to hold your full motorcycle licence from years ago it's recommended that you seek refresher training before taking to the road on a modern motorcycle.

Most Approved Training Bodies (ATBs) can provide this training and it's a good way to refresh your skills in a safe and enjoyable manner.

You can find a local ATB from

- Yellow Pages or local newspapers
- your motorcycle dealer
- the internet.

The Enhanced Rider Scheme

DSA, in conjunction with the Motorcycle Training Industry and leading Insurance Companies, have devised a new package of training known as the Enhanced Rider Scheme (ERS).

The scheme is intended to benefit all bike riders who have a full motorcycle licence, irrespective of experience including those who have just passed their test. Those who undertake the training will receive insurance discounts from those Insurance Companies who have signed up to the scheme.

Trainers who deliver the Enhanced Rider Scheme must be registered with DSA on its Register of Post-test Motorcycle Trainers (RPMT).

To find out more about ERS or to look for an RPMT trainer in your area visit www.transportoffice.gov.uk

Motorcycle technology is constantly changing, as a returning rider give yourself some time to become used to your new machine

Motorcycles don't have very big fuel tanks compared to cars and this can lead to surprisingly frequent stops for fuel

Budgeting

Motorcycling is traditionally a cheap form of transport, but running some modern motorcycles can be more expensive than running some types of car. If you're a beginner you must accept that there are considerable start-up costs.

Don't cut costs to below the minimum level of safety. For example, don't risk using worn or damaged tyres. Safety must never be sacrificed for economy.

Set yourself a budget so that you know what you can afford. This will help you to identify where savings can be made.

You'll have to consider the

- purchase price of the motorcycle
- vehicle excise duty and insurance
- cost of proper clothing and a safety helmet
- cost of training
- running costs: fuel, maintenance, etc.

section **two**
THE RIDER AND THE LAW

This section covers

- Motorcycle riders
- Moped riders
- Compulsory Basic Training
- Foreign licence holders
- Disqualified riders
- New drivers act
- Vehicle documents
- Insurance

Motorcycle riders

You have to comply with certain legal requirements before you can ride on the road. Most of the requirements are there to protect you and other road users. If you neglect them you could face serious penalties.

To ride a motorcycle on the road you must be at least 17 years old and hold a driving licence that allows you to ride motorcycles (Category A). That licence can be any of the following

- a provisional driving licence. This provides provisional car, motorcycle and moped entitlement
- a full category A motorcycle licence
- a full sub-category A1 light motorcycle licence
- a full car licence. This provides provisional motorcycle entitlement
- a full moped licence. This provides provisional motorcycle entitlement.

All riders must

- wear a safety helmet at all times when riding unless they are a member of the Sikh religion and wear a turban
- ensure any helmet visor used conforms to BSI or EU standards.

Provisional motorcycle entitlement

After completing Compulsory Basic Training (CBT) (see Compulsory Basic Training later in this section) learners may ride a solo motorcycle

- up to 125 cc
- with a power output of no more than 11 kW.

Provisional driving licences will be issued with provisional motorcycle entitlement valid for the life of the licence (subject to holding a valid CBT certificate).

Am I required to take a theory test?

All practical motorcycle test candidates must first pass a motorcycle theory test, unless they are upgrading from A1 to A or they hold a full moped licence which was obtained by passing the moped test after 1 July 1996.

Where can I get a driving licence application form?

Forms are available from

- Post Offices
- Traffic Area Offices
- Vehicle Registration Offices
- Driver and Vehicle Licensing Agency
- www.direct.gov.uk/motoring

Learners who wish to ride a sidecar outfit can do so as long as it has a power to weight ratio not exceeding 0.16 kW/kg.

With provisional motorcycle entitlement you must not

- ride on motorways
- carry a pillion passenger
- ride without red L-plates fitted to both front and rear of the motorcycle. In Wales you may display red D-plates (for dysgwr, the Welsh for 'learner'). If you cross from Wales into another part of the United Kingdom you must display L-plates.

Full motorcycle licence

There are two types of full motorcycle licence; sub-category A1 – light motorcycle licence and category A – standard motorcycle licence.

Sub-category A1

A full A1 licence allows you to ride machines up to 125 cc and with a power output of up to 11 kW (14.6 bhp).

You can obtain a full sub-category A1 licence by passing the practical test on a bike of between 75 cc and 125 cc.

Category A

A full category A licence gives you full entitlement to all machines.

You can obtain a full category A licence

- with a two-year qualifying period
- without a two-year qualifying period via Direct Access (see below).

Category A with 2 year qualifying period - This will be obtained by passing the motorcycle test on a motorcycle of between 121 cc and 125 cc and capable of at least 100 km/h (62.5 mph).

Riders who are subject to the two-year qualifying period will be restricted to machines of 25 kW (33 bhp) maximum and a power to weight ratio not exceeding 0.16 kW/kg for two years from the date of passing their test. At the end of that time any size of motorcycle may be ridden without taking another test.

Category A via Direct Access - This is for riders aged 21 or over. Passing the motorcycle test on a machine of at least 35 kW (46.6 bhp) gives immediate access to all sizes of motorcycle.

You can practise on any size of motorcycle which exceeds the UK learner specification provided that

- you're accompanied at all times by a qualified approved trainer, on another motorcycle and in radio contact
- fluorescent or reflective safety clothing is worn during supervision
- L-plates (D-plates in Wales) are fitted and provisional licence restrictions followed.

Accelerated Access - This option is for riders over 21 years old or who reach the age of 21 before their two-year qualifying period is complete.

You can take a further test to give you immediate access to all motorcycles. This test must be taken on a motorcycle with a power output of at least 35 kW (46.6 bhp).

To practice for this test you're restricted to the same conditions as for Direct Access (see above).

Full licence entitlement

With a full motorcycle licence you may

- ride without L-plates (or D-plates in Wales)
- carry a pillion passenger
- use motorways.

Moped riders

To ride a moped on the road you must be at least 16 years old and have a licence that entitles you to ride mopeds (Category P).

At 16 but under 17 this can be a

- provisional moped licence
- full moped licence

> **Remember,** a moped must not be ridden on motorways, even if you hold a full licence.

At 17 and over it can also be a

- full car licence (see page 23)
- full motorcycle licence
- provisional driving licence. This provides provisional moped entitlement.

Provisional moped entitlement

After completing CBT this allows you to ride a moped. You must not

- carry a pillion passenger.
- ride without L-plates (or D-plates in Wales) fitted to both the front and the rear of the moped
- ride on motorways.

Full moped licence

Full moped entitlement allows you to

- ride mopeds without L-plates
- carry a pillion passenger.

What defines a moped?

A moped must have an engine capacity under 50 cc and not weigh more than 250 kg.

If it was registered after 1 August 1977, it's maximum design speed cannot exceed 50 km/h (about 32 mph). Mopeds built after June 2003 are restricted to 45 km/h (28mph).

Are there any moped validation restrictions?

If training is completed on a motorcycle-sidecar combination or on a moped that has more than two wheels

- moped validation will be limited to mopeds with more than two wheels

- motorcycle validation will be limited to motorcycle-sidecar combinations.

Full car licence holders

Holders of a full car licence obtained by passing their driving test before 1 February 2001 hold unconditional full moped entitlement.

Holders of a full car licence obtained by passing their driving test on or after 1 February 2001, who do not already hold a full moped or motorcycle licence, must hold a valid CBT completion certificate (DL196) to validate their full moped entitlement.

Remember, the same DL196 that validates your full moped entitlement will have a limited life (see Certificate life) for validating provisional motorcycle entitlement.

If a valid DL196 is already held when the car test is passed, the full moped entitlement will be validated immediately.

A DL196 validating full moped entitlement on a full car licence will remain valid for mopeds, for the life of the licence. It is therefore particularly important that the DL196 is kept safe.

Compulsory Basic Training

All learner motorcycle and moped riders must complete a course of Compulsory Basic Training (CBT) before riding on the road. CBT can only be given by Approved Training Bodies (ATBs) who have

- trainers that have been assessed by DSA
- sites approved by DSA for off-road training.

CBT allows you to safely learn

- motorcycling theory
- skills which will make you safe on the road
- the correct attitude.

Many people find CBT is an enjoyable activity and an opportunity to meet like-minded motorcyclists.

You don't have to take CBT if you

- passed a full moped test after 1 December 1990
- live and ride on specified offshore islands
- already hold a full licence for another category in A.

When you've completed CBT you'll be given a DL196. Keep this safe. You must have a DL196 before you can take the practical motorcycle test.

CBT may be taken on a Direct Access motorcycle. Some of the initial parts however, may be covered around a standard learner machine.

CBT Certificates (DL196)

CBT may be completed on

- a moped or motorcycle
- a motorcycle-sidecar combination or moped that has more than two wheels.

The DL196 will record whether CBT was completed on a two-wheeled machine or one with more than two wheels and will validate provisional entitlement accordingly.

Certificate life - CBT certificates have a two-year life. A certificate validating full moped entitlement on a full car licence will remain valid for mopeds, for the life of the licence.

Foreign licence holders

Visitors or new residents

Visitors to Great Britain or new residents can drive on their foreign licence or International Driving Permit (IDP) for up to 12 months.

You must make sure that

- your licence or IDP is valid
- you have entitlement for the size of motorcycle you intend to ride
- you're aged 17 or over.

You must apply for a UK licence before riding if

- you don't have the correct motorcycle entitlement
- you've been in Great Britain for more than 12 months.

If you want to take a motorcycle test you'll have to hold a UK provisional licence before you take

- the theory test
- the practical motorcycle test.

European Community and other driving licences

EC licences are valid for driving in the UK until they expire. Licences from designated countries can be exchanged for a UK licence within 12 months without the need to take a test.

If, however, your motorcycle entitlement was granted automatically when you passed a test in a car or other vehicle

- you'll be given full moped entitlement and provisional motorcycle entitlement
- you'll have to pass a motorcycle test to have full motorcycle entitlement.

Information Leaflet D100, 'What you need to know about driving licences' gives further information about foreign licences available for exchange.

This is available at larger Post Offices or you can get further advice from

The Driver Enquiry Unit,
The Driver and Vehicle Licensing Agency (DVLA), Swansea SA6 7JL

Telephone: 0870 240 0009
or visit www.dvla.gov.uk

How to obtain a full motorcycle licence

Type of licence currently held	CBT required?
Provisional driving licence	Yes, before you can ride on the road
Full car licence	Yes, before you can ride on the road
Full motorcycle licence (category A), and subject to the two-year qualifying period	No
Full motorcycle licence (sub-category A1)	No
Full moped licence, obtained by passing a moped test after 1 July 1996	No
Full moped licence, obtained by passing a moped test between 1 December 1990 and 1 July 1996	No
Full moped licence, obtained by passing a moped test before 1 December 1990	Yes, before you can ride a motorcycle on the road

How to obtain a full moped licence

Provisional moped licence (aged 16)	Yes, before you can ride on the road
Provisional driving licence	Yes, before you can ride on the road

How to validate full moped entitlement on a full car licence...

Full car licence obtained by passing the driving test after 1 February 2001	Yes. DL196 remains valid for the life of the licence

Minimum test vehicles

Minimum test vehicles	Engine
Moped	Under 50 cc
Light motorcycle (A1)	75–125 cc
Standard motorcycle	121–125 cc
Accelerated access	Unspecified
Direct access	Unspecified

Theory test required?	Direct access	Accelerated access
Yes, before you take the practical test	Must be 21 or over	Not applicable
Yes, before you take the practical test	Must be 21 or over	Not applicable
No	Not applicable	Available if you're aged 21 or over
No	Must be 21 or over	Not applicable
No	Must be 21 or over	Not applicable
Yes, before you take the practical test	Must be 21 or over	Not applicable
Yes, before you take the practical test	Must be 21 or over	Not applicable
Yes, before you take the practical moped test	Not applicable	Not applicable
Yes, before you take the practical moped test	Not applicable	Not applicable
issued after 1 February 2001		
No	Not applicable	Not applicable

Minimum test vehicles

Power	Speed
-	See page 23 for details
11 kW (14.6 bhp) maximum	If between 121–125 cc and can exceed 100 km/h (62.5 mph) a category A will be given
11 kW (14.6 bhp) maximum	Capable of exceeding 100 km/h (62.5 mph)
35 kW (46.6 bhp) minimum	Unspecified
35 kW (46.6 bhp) minimum	Unspecified

Disqualified riders

Tough penalties exist for anyone convicted of dangerous riding or driving.

Courts will impose an extended test on anyone convicted of dangerous driving offences. They can also impose an extended test on anyone convicted of other offences involving obligatory disqualification.

If you've been disqualified for other endorsable offences the courts can order a normal-length test before you can recover a full licence.

Recovering a full licence

A rider subject to a retest can apply for a provisional licence at the end of the disqualification period. The normal rules for provisional licence holders will apply.

The theory test must be passed before applying for either an extended or a normal-length test.

CBT

If you have been disqualified your DL196 is rendered invalid by the disqualification, and CBT will have to be retaken.

The extended test

The extended motorcycle or moped test involves about 70 minutes' riding time. The test routes cover a wide variety of roads, usually including dual carriageways.

A rider has to

- maintain a satisfactory standard throughout the extended test period
- cope with a wide range of road and traffic conditions.

The examiner will apply the same standard of assessment as for an ordinary test. However, the extra time and wide variety of road and traffic conditions make the extended test more demanding. Candidates should make sure that they're well prepared before applying.

Higher fees - The higher fee for the extended motorcycle test reflects the extra length of the test.

New drivers act

How you may be affected

Special rules apply for the first two years after the date of passing your first practical test.

Your licence will be revoked if the number of penalty points on your licence reaches six or more as a result of offences you commit before the two years are over. Offences you committed before passing your test will be taken into account.

You must then reapply for a provisional licence. CBT will have to be completed again and all learner restrictions will apply until you pass the theory and practical test again.

This applies even if you pay by fixed penalty.

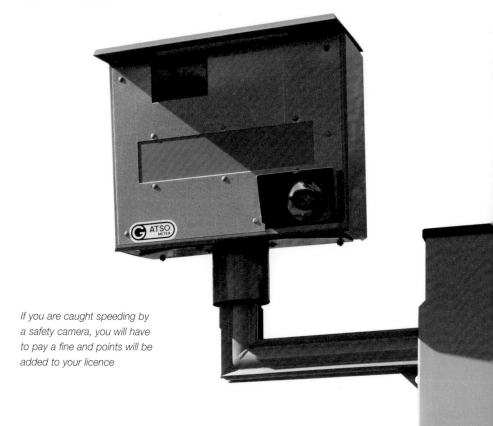

If you are caught speeding by a safety camera, you will have to pay a fine and points will be added to your licence

Vehicle documents

The Vehicle Registration Certificate (V5C)

A Registration Certificate shows the registered keeper of a vehicle.

It gives the keeper's name and address and information about the vehicle including the make, model, engine size and the date it was first registered. A new Registration Certificate is issued each time DVLA updates the record with any change to the existing details.

> **Remember,** the registered keeper is the person who keeps the vehicle on a public road. They are not necessarily the legal owner and a Registration Certificate is not proof of ownership.

If you buy a new vehicle - your dealer will see that you get one of these certificates.

If you buy a second-hand vehicle - make sure you're given the document. You shouldn't buy a vehicle without a Registration Certificate. This document is a good indication that the vehicle hasn't been stolen.

Updating and replacing - It's your legal responsibility to keep the details of your Vehicle Registration Certificate up to date. If you move house or change your name, let DVLA know, otherwise you may have problems when you come to sell or relicense your vehicle.

You can update your details by filling in the relevant section of your Registration Certificate and sending it to DVLA. They will then send you an updated version free of charge.

If you lose or mislay your Registration Certificate, you can request a replacement from DVLA. If you are the registered keeper and there are no changes to your personal or vehicle details, fill in application form V62, or call 0870 240 0010. There's a fee for all replacement certificates.

Vehicle excise duty

You can buy a tax disc (vehicle licence) for six or twelve months. The tax disc must be displayed on the vehicle. Any vehicle exempt from duty must display a 'Nil' tax disc. A tax disc must not be transferred to another vehicle.

New Excise Duty Rules - Since 1 January 2004 the registered keeper of a vehicle (the person named on DVLA's record) remains responsible for taxing a vehicle or making a SORN (Statutory Off Road Notification) until that liability is formally transferred to a new keeper.

The keeper needs to inform DVLA when the vehicle is off the road, or has been sold, transferred, scrapped or exported or they remain liable for taxing it. Once DVLA has been notified about a sale/transfer or that the vehicle is off-road they will issue an acknowledgement letter, which should be kept as proof that the vehicle record has been changed.

If you don't re-license your vehicle - Keepers who fail to re-license their vehicle (or declare SORN) will incur an automatic penalty. DVLA will carry out a computer check each month to identify those vehicles without a valid tax disc. Although it is no longer necessary for the vehicle to be seen on a public road before a penalty is issued, on-road enforcement will still continue.

To display your motorcycle's tax disc use a weatherproof tax disc holder and fix it securely in a convenient place

To ensure your tax disc is up to date - Fill in the relevant section of the renewal reminder form V11, or apply for a new tax disc by filling in form V10. You will also need to produce your Vehicle Registration Certificate (or the tear-off slip V5/2-V5C/2 if within 2 months of date of purchase).

In both cases take the completed form to a licence-issuing Post Office to obtain your tax disc. You will also need to produce

- a valid certificate of insurance
- an MOT certificate if the vehicle is over 3 years old (some vehicles may be covered by other requirements).

Excise duty rates - These classes are

- up to 150 cc
- 151–250 cc
- over 250 cc.

Statutory Off Road Notification (SORN) - If you don't intend to use or keep the vehicle on a public road, you can declare SORN and then you don't have to pay road tax. Your SORN declaration is valid for 12 months (provided the vehicle is kept off-road). Failure to renew it (or re-license) will incur a penalty.

You can declare SORN by

- filling in the relevant section of your renewal reminder form V11 and taking it to a licence-issuing Post Office branch
- calling 0870 240 0010, if you are the registered keeper
- filling in a SORN declaration form V890 and sending it to DVLA. These forms are available from all DVLA Local Offices, licence-issuing Post Office branches or by downloading from www.dvla.gov.uk
- making a declaration on 'application for refund' forms V14 and V33 if you are also applying for a refund and the vehicle is to remain in your possession.

Older motorcycles - Older motorcycles may be classed as 'historic' and as such are exempt from vehicle excise duty. If you have an older motorcycle check with DVLA to find out if it qualifies. Remember, all motorcycles must display a valid tax disc, even if no fee is payable.

The vehicle test certificate

The MOT test applies to all motor vehicles three years old and over.

The purpose of the MOT test is to ensure that your vehicle's key safety and environmental systems and components meet the required minimum legal standards.

The test must be carried out every year by a Vehicle Testing Station appointed by the Vehicle Inspectorate, an executive agency of the Department for Transport.

Vehicles which must be tested - If your motorcycle is more than three years old you must have a current MOT test certificate. You won't be able to renew your Vehicle Excise Licence without it.

Testing time - You can have it tested as much as one month before the current certificate runs out. The expiry date of the new certificate will be one year after the expiry date of the old one.

> **Remember,** an MOT test certificate is not a guarantee that the vehicle will remain roadworthy and comply with the minimum standards of the certificate. Neither does it imply that the engine and transmission systems are in good condition.

Failure - If your vehicle fails and you want to continue to use it, you must make arrangements to have the necessary repairs carried out without delay. The vehicle must pass a retest before it's used on the road except when

- driving it away from the testing station after failing the test
- driving to have the repairs carried out
- driving to an MOT test appointment booked in advance.

Even in these circumstances you can still be prosecuted if your car is not roadworthy under the various regulations governing its construction and use. In addition, check that your insurance cover remains valid.

Appeals - Details giving information on the right to appeal if you consider the vehicle has been incorrectly failed may be obtained at Vehicle Testing Stations.

Fees - Ask any Vehicle Testing Station about the current test and retest fees.

Insurance

It's illegal to ride without insurance. Should you cause injury to anyone or damage property it could result in prosecution.

Before you take a motorcycle onto public roads get proper insurance cover. You can arrange this through

- the insurance company directly
- a broker
- a motorcycle dealer
- the manufacturer (sometimes)

The insurance company - Insuring directly with an insurance company is probably a little cheaper than the same policy through a broker. Finding the best deal, however, can be a time consuming business.

A broker - Many brokers are linked by computer to the main insurance companies. This allows them to get comparative quotes very quickly. A good broker will shop around and find the best policy for you.

If you already have car insurance ask your present insurer first.

A motorcycle dealer - A dealer can act as a broker or may have a direct link with an insurance company. Sometimes the dealer can offer insurance deals through the manufacturers.

The manufacturer - Some larger manufacturers make arrangements with insurance companies. This benefits the motorcyclist by offering competitive rates. Your dealer will be able to tell you about cover in this category.

Types of insurance

Third party - This type of insurance is the legal minimum and the cheapest cover. The 'third party' is any person you might injure or property you might damage. You aren't covered for damage to your motorcycle or injury to yourself.

If you damage another vehicle the owner could claim against your insurance. On the other hand, if someone damaged your motorcycle you could claim against them.

Third party, fire and theft - This is the same as third party but it also covers you for

- your motorcycle being stolen
- damage by fire.

Comprehensive - This is the best, but the most expensive insurance. Apart from covering other persons and property from injury and damage this also covers damage to your machine.

Pillion passenger insurance - All policies include cover for a pillion passenger. This is much the same as for car passengers.

Cost of insurance

This varies with

- your age – the younger you are, the more it will cost
- the make of your motorcycle
- the power and capacity of the engine
- where you live.

Engine-size groups for insurance purposes can vary from one insurer to another. This is another reason to shop around when looking for insurance cover.

What's insured

This also varies from company to company. Read the small print and ask your insurer or broker. You'll often have to pay the first £50 or £100 of any claim. This is called the 'excess'.

Shop around and buy the best policy you can afford.

Certificate of insurance

This is a simple document that certifies

- who is insured
- the type of vehicle covered
- the kind of insurance cover
- the period of cover
- the main conditions.

Sometimes a broker will give you a temporary certificate or 'cover note'. This is issued while you're waiting for your certificate and is proof of insurance. Keep the certificate safe. You'll need to produce it if the police ask you and when you apply to renew your vehicle excise licence.

The policy document

This contains the full details of the contract between you and the insurance company. It's usually written in legal language. Ask your broker or the insurance company to explain anything you don't understand.

section **three**
CHOOSING A MOTORCYCLE

This section covers
- Buying a motorcycle
- Types of motorcycle

Buying a motorcycle

Motorcycles come in many different types and sizes. The various types of motorcycle and their main features are described over the next few pages. You need to think carefully before deciding which one to buy.

Apart from buying the machine you'll have to consider insurance, running costs and clothing.

You'll also need to consider your budget, the location of the nearest dealer and where to get advice if you need it.

You can get further information from manufacturers' brochures, magazines and newspapers. Talking to other riders can give you another viewpoint. However, at the end of the day, the final choice is always yours.

Budgeting

Costs you'll have to think about include

- purchase price. This may determine whether you buy new or second-hand
- insurance. Some models cost a lot more to insure than others
- running costs. Fuel consumption, tyres and the cost of spare parts need to be considered
- clothing. If you're new to motorcycling the cost of a helmet, gloves, jacket, boots, etc. can be a major consideration.

Type of motorcycle

When choosing a machine you'll need to ask yourself about

- **your licence** - Are you entitled to ride motorcycles of any engine size?
- **suitability** - What do you want from your motorcycle? A small commuter machine is going to struggle with long-distance motorway riding
- **comfort** - Are you comfortable on the machine? Can you reach the controls easily? Can your feet reach the ground?
- **weight** - Some motorcycles are very heavy. This can present problems when parking or manoeuvring.

Motorcycle dealers

The motorcycle dealership in your area could influence your decision. Being able to have your machine serviced locally could be important to you. A dealer can also

- offer finance packages
- offer part exchange deals
- offer special insurance rates
- arrange training courses
- let you try out a motorcycle before you make a final decision (subject to your licence entitlement)
- give you expert advice.

Types of motorcycle

Mopeds

A moped is a motorcycle which

- must not have an engine capacity over 50 cc
- has a restricted maximum speed (see page 22)
- doesn't weigh more than 250 kg
- can be moved by pedals, if the moped was registered before 1 August 1977.

A moped can be ridden without L- plates (or D-plates in Wales) by people who hold a full car, moped or motorcycle licence. Full car licence holders who passed their test on or after 1 February 2001 must complete CBT to validate their full moped entitlement. See Section Two.

Light motorcycles

These motorcycles are suitable for use by learners provided

- the engine isn't over 125 cc
- the engine power output doesn't exceed 11 kW (14.6 bhp)
- L-plates (or D-plates in Wales) are fitted both to the front and back of the machine.

These engine size restrictions don't apply to learners under the accelerated or direct access schemes. See Section Two.

Automatic motorcycles

Automatic or semi-automatic motorcycles have automatic transmission. They're usually small and easy to ride. You can take your motorcycle test on one of these machines. If you pass your full licence entitlement will be restricted to such machines.

Automatic motorcycles are ideal for short trips and for use in heavy town traffic.

Mid-range motorcycles

These are good all rounder machines equally suitable for commuting to work or for longer trips. They are comfortable to ride and are quite capable of travelling up to all the legal speed limits.

Machines of this type are generally used for direct or accelerated access training courses provided their engine's power output meets the legal minimum of 35 kW (46.6 bhp) .

Sports motorcycles

These motorcycles have road racing styling. They come in a variety of engine sizes and can be

- expensive to buy and run
- capable of very high speed.

When you ride this type of machine for the first time, take care. You may find yourself going faster than you intended.

Touring motorcycles

Touring motorcycles are designed for comfortable long distance riding. They feature

- a relaxed riding position
- luggage carrying capacity
- often some form of fairing for weather protection
- a large engine.

Despite their size and weight these motorcycles are capable of continuous travel at motorway speeds.

Custom motorcycles

Sometimes called 'cruisers', these motorcycles are recognisable by their unique styling. They

- are available in a wide range of engine sizes, including 125 cc
- usually have a low seat height
- have a 'laid back' riding position.

Off-road motorcycles (trail bikes)

Trail bikes are designed so that they can be used both on and off the road. This type of motorcycle

- comes in a wide range of engine sizes
- has extra ground clearance, which increases the seat height
- is fitted with dual purpose tyres
- is built to cope with riding over rough ground.

section **four**
CLOTHING AND PROTECTION

This section covers

- Visors and goggles
- Safety helmets
- Protective clothing
- Gloves and gauntlets
- Boots
- Visibility aids
- Motorcycle fairings

Visors and goggles

A visor or goggles are vital to protect your eyes from wind, rain, insects and road dirt.

All visors and goggles must

- comply with British Standard
  - BS 4110 Grade X, or
  - BS 4110 Grade XA, or
  - BS 4110 Grade YA, or
  - BS 4110 Grade ZA
- display a BSI kitemark or
- comply with a European standard which offers a level of safety and protection at least equivalent to these British Standards and carry a mark equivalent to the BSI kitemark (ECE 22-05).

Goggles may comply with the EU Directive on Personal Protective Equipment and carry the 'CE' mark.

Glasses and tinted eyewear

If you normally wear glasses or contact lenses you must by law wear them when you ride. Don't wear tinted glasses, visors or goggles if you're riding in the dark or in conditions of poor visibility.

Cleaning your visor or goggles

It's very important that you keep your visor or goggles clean. You must have a clear view of the road ahead at all times. To clean your goggles or visor wash them in warm soapy water. Don't use solvents or petrol.

In cold and wet weather your visor or goggles might fog up on the inside. You can use a special anti-fog spray to help prevent this. If your visor or goggles fog up when you're riding choose somewhere safe to stop, and wipe them with a clean cloth. Carry a cloth with you for this purpose.

Damaged or scratched goggles and visors

Scratches on your visor or goggles can distort your view and cause dazzle from the lights of oncoming vehicles at night. It can cause glare, especially from low winter sun.

If your visor or goggles are heavily scratched renew them.

Safety helmets

By law, you must wear a safety helmet when riding a motorcycle on the road (members of the Sikh religion who wear a turban are exempt).

All helmets sold in the UK must either

- comply with British Standard BS 6658: 1985 and carry the BSI kitemark, or
- comply with UNECE Regulation 22.05 (it will be marked with a UN 'E' mark - the first two digits of the approval number will be '05'), or
- comply with any standard accepted by a member of the European Economic Area (EEA State) which offers a level of safety and protection equivalent to BS 6658: 1985 and carry a mark equivalent to the BSI kitemark.

From spring 2008, SHARP (Safety Helmet and Assessment Rating Programme) will offer you a single, easy-to-understand rating for helmets. To find out more, visit http://sharp.direct.gov.uk/

Types of safety helmet

Motorcycle helmets are either full-face, or open-face.

Full-face helmets - This type of helmet

- covers the head fully and has a hinged visor
- protects the face in an accident
- offers more weather protection than an open-face helmet.

Open-face helmets - This type of helmet is preferred by riders who feel closed in by full-face helmets and can be worn with either a visor or goggles. However, it doesn't protect the chin in an accident.

Flip-up helmets - These are open face helmets with a hinged front that closes to resemble a full-face helmet. The visor can be opened or closed independent of the hinged front. Make sure that you lock the chin guard down before riding.

Helmet fit

When you buy a new helmet it should be a good, snug fit. The padding will soon bed down and this could make the helmet loose. A loose helmet isn't only uncomfortable, it could also come off in an accident.

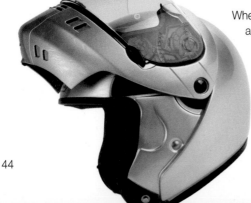

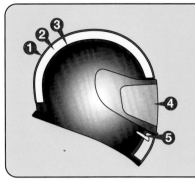

1. **Outer shell** - Designed to disperse the power of an impact in the event of an accident.

2. **Crumple zone** - This expanded polystyrene layer is designed to absorb the remaining impact.

3. **Comfort layer** - Comprised of different types of foams which provides a comfortable fit.

4. **Visor** - Made from strong polycarbonate, it protects the rider's face.

5. **Ventilation** - Supplies a source of fresh air and helps to remove exhaled humidity.

Helmet fastening

Helmets usually use one of three different fastening methods; double D-ring, quick release and bar and buckle. Some helmet straps also have a velcro tab to secure the strap so that it doesn't flap in the wind. It isn't to be used to fasten the helmet.

It is both unsafe and illegal to ride with a helmet unfastened or incorrectly fastened.

Helmet materials

The outer shell of motorcycle safety helmets are made in three basic materials - polycarbonate, glass fibre and kelvar.

Polycarbonate

- lighter than glass fibre
- must not be painted or have stickers affixed
- must not be cleaned with solvents.

Polycarbonate helmets tend to be cheaper than other types and don't last as long.

Glass fibre

- heavier than polycarbonate
- lasts longer than polycarbonate
- easy to clean.

Kevlar

- extremely tough
- used as a composite with glass fibre, or carbon and glass fibre
- combines great strength with light weight
- tends to be expensive.

Damage to helmets

If your helmet receives any serious impact buy a new one. Damage won't always be visible to the naked eye. For this reason never use a second-hand helmet. A damaged helmet could be unreliable in an accident. Repairs to damaged helmets are not recommended.

Protective clothing

Clothing is available which will keep you warm and dry in all but the worst conditions. If you allow yourself to become cold and wet when riding you'll lose concentration.

Protective clothing for motorcyclists is designed to protect you from

- the cold and wet
- some kinds of injury.

Clothing for which a manufacturer either claims or implies protection, other than from the weather, must be marked with the 'CE' mark.

Motorcycle protective clothing is of two main types

- clothing made from man-made materials
- leather clothing.

Man-made materials

To protect you from the weather, nylon is the most popular material. It's available in many different forms and comes under many different brand names. Other materials such as waxed cotton and PVC are also available.

More expensive garments have reinforcing and padding at the shoulders and elbows. This provides some protection in the event of an accident.

Generally, man-made outer clothing is designed to fit over your normal clothes and comes as a jacket and trousers or a one-piece suit. They are available lined or unlined.

When you're buying outer clothing make sure that you have enough room for extra layers of warm clothing underneath and that your movement isn't restricted.

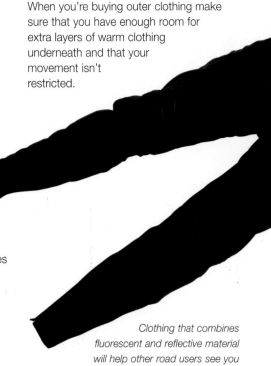

Clothing that combines fluorescent and reflective material will help other road users see you during the day and at night

Leathers

Motorcyclists have traditionally worn leathers. They offer a high degree of protection from abrasion if you fall off. Motorcycle leathers come in several different types.

One-piece suits - Leather motorcycle suits aren't designed to fit over your normal clothes. They do, however, offer the motorcyclist certain advantages including reduced wind resistance and a high degree of windproofing.

They also have some disadvantages. For a start, they are expensive to buy.

Leathers are only showerproof (you'll have to use a waterproof oversuit in wet weather) and they are not warm. Due to the close fit, you can't wear extra layers underneath in cold weather and you may experience some restriction of movement.

Two-piece zip-together suits - These comprise a separate jacket and trousers which zip together. This style has some advantages:

- you can buy the jacket or trousers separately. This lets you spread the cost to suit your budget. It also lets you buy different sizes to suit you
- zipping the jacket and trousers together helps to stop draughts around your waist
- jacket or trousers can be worn separately.

Separate jacket and trousers - This option

- is often the least expensive
- gives you a wide choice of styles, colours, sizes and prices.

When you are choosing leathers look for additional protection for shoulders, elbows and knees.

Visit your motorcycle dealer or motorcycle clothing supplier. Try on various types of clothing for fit and comfort. As a general rule, buy the best you can afford.

Gloves and gauntlets

Good gloves or gauntlets are essential when you ride a motorcycle. Never be tempted to ride without gloves. If you fall off you could seriously injure your hands. Your gloves should

- protect your hands from cold and wet weather
- protect your hands if you fall off
- allow you to operate the controls easily.

Gauntlets prevent wind and rain from being driven up your sleeves. However, in heavy rain the water can sometimes run down your sleeves into your gloves. Modern motorcycle gauntlets have adjustable cuffs to help overcome this problem.

Materials

Leather is the most suitable material for motorcycle gloves. On its own it's tough, supple and resistant to water, but when combined with modern materials and construction methods it can be used to make waterproof gloves. Gloves made from cheaper materials don't provide the same level of protection. For protection from prolonged rain you may need to wear overmitts.

Overmitts

Overmitts prevent gloves from becoming sodden in prolonged wet weather riding. You wear them over your usual motorcycle gloves or gauntlets. They are made from waterproof material, either waxed cotton or nylon. Make sure that you can operate the controls properly when wearing overmitts.

Cold

When riding in very cold weather your hands can become painfully cold. No matter how good your gloves, the cold will eventually get through. This in turn can cause you to lose concentration when riding.

To overcome the cold you can try wearing thin inner gloves. Experiment with various combinations to find one that suits you.

Heated gloves and handlebar grips

If you're serious about motorcycling in cold weather then you'll need either

- electrically heated inner gloves
- electrically heated handlebar grips.

These accessories put a large demand on your motorcycle's electrical generator. Check that it can cope with the extra demands before you buy and fit them.

Boots

It's important to wear good boots or stout footwear when you ride a motorcycle. If you wear sandals or trainers your feet will have little protection if you fall off.

Motorcycle boots

- protect your feet from cold and wet weather
- offer some protection if you have an accident
- protect your feet and shins from knocks and bumps.

Types of boots

There are three types of motorcycle boots

- leather
- rubber
- plastic.

Leather boots - Leather is strong, flexible and weather resistant. This makes it the most suitable material for motorcycle boots. Leather boots give the best protection in the event of an accident.

Boots made from leather combined with modern materials and construction techniques can resist water, even in the wettest conditions. However, leather alone isn't totally waterproof and you might need to wear overboots in very wet weather.

Leather boots are available either unlined or lined with warm fleece material.

Rubber or plastic boots - Rubber or plastic boots are waterproof and cheaper than leather. You can buy them lined or unlined, and leather-look boots are also available.

Whichever type of boot you decide to buy make sure that

- they're comfortable
- you can operate the foot controls easily.

Try as many different boots as you can and always buy the best you can afford.

Cold

Your feet can become very cold when you're riding in wintery conditions.

Wearing an extra pair of socks can help. If your feet become too cold stop and warm up before continuing your journey.

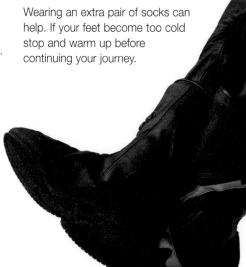

Visibility aids

Many road accidents involving motorcyclists occur because another road user didn't see them. Using some form of visibility aid will help others to see you.

In daylight

Wearing fluorescent orange or yellow clothing will improve your chances of being seen. This can be

- a fluorescent jacket
- a fluorescent tabard or waistcoat
- a 'Sam Browne' belt.

You need to be visible from the side as well as the front and back.

Other methods you could use to help other road users to see you in daylight include

- wearing a white or brightly coloured helmet and coloured clothing
- having your headlamp on dipped beam.

In the dark

To improve visibility in the dark you need to wear reflective material. This can be reflective belts, patches or strips. They work by reflecting the light from headlamps of other vehicles. This makes you much more visible from a long distance away.

Reflective strips on your gloves will help other road users to see your arm signals.

Motorcycle fairings

Motorcycle fairings come in three main types

- handlebar fairings
- touring fairings
- sports fairings.

Handlebar fairings

These protect your hands and body and are available in either sports or touring styles.

Touring fairings

These provide weather protection to the hands, legs and feet. They also make high-speed riding more comfortable by keeping you out of the wind.

Sports fairings

These give some weather protection but they're mainly intended to cut down wind resistance.

Windscreens

These protect your face and body from the wind and rain.

Handlebar muffs

Handlebar muffs are designed to keep the wind and rain off your hands.

A typical touring fairing

A typical sports fairing

51

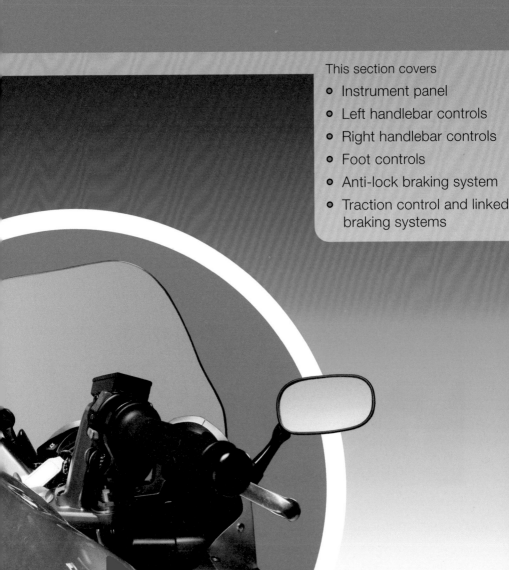

section **five**
MOTORCYCLE CONTROLS

This section covers

- Instrument panel
- Left handlebar controls
- Right handlebar controls
- Foot controls
- Anti-lock braking system
- Traction control and linked braking systems

Instrument panel

Speedometer

Tells you how fast you're going in miles per hour and kilometres per hour.

Mileometer (odometer)

Usually housed in the speedometer. It shows an overall total of how many miles or kilometres your motorcycle has covered.

Temperature gauge

Fitted to motorcycles with liquid cooled engines. It shows the coolant temperature and warns if the engine is overheating.

Rev. counter

Shows the engine speed in revolutions (revs) per minute.

Ignition lamp

Comes on when you switch on the ignition. It should go out when the engine is running. If it doesn't, this shows a problem with the battery charging system.

Neutral lamp

Glows to tell you when the gear selector is in the neutral position.

High beam lamp

Indicates when your headlamp is on high beam.

Oil pressure lamp

Warns you of low oil pressure. If it comes on when the engine is running, you may have a serious problem. Stop the engine immediately and investigate the cause.

Indicator repeater

Tells you that your indicators are in use. Use it to check if you've cancelled a signal.

Left handlebar controls

Headlamp flasher

This switch lets you flash your headlamp. This has the same meaning as sounding your horn. Flash your headlamp if your horn may not be heard, for example on the motorway.

Horn

Sound the horn to warn other road users if you don't think they've seen you.

You must not sound your horn

- between 11.30 pm and 7 am in a built-up area
- when your motorcycle is stationary, unless a moving vehicle poses a danger.

Headlamp dip switch

Lets you switch your headlamp between main beam and dipped beam.

On main beam you'll usually see a blue warning lamp on your instrument panel. At night, switch to dipped beam when meeting or following other vehicles. This will stop you dazzling other drivers.

Indicators

You use the indicators to let other road users know that you intend to change direction. You must make sure that you cancel them after turning.

Clutch lever

Operates the clutch, which engages and disengages the engine from the drive to the rear wheel. Use the clutch

- when you select first gear before moving off
- to prevent the engine stalling when you stop
- to help change gears
- when selecting neutral.

To change or select a gear

- pull the clutch lever fully to the handlebar
- select the gear you need
- release the clutch lever smoothly to engage the clutch.

Fully automatic motorcycles - This type of motorcycle has no clutch lever. Often the rear brake lever is fitted in place of the clutch lever.

Semi-automatic motorcycles - These have no clutch lever. The clutch operates automatically when you use the gear-change pedal.

Choke

A device which helps when starting a cold engine. It operates by changing the amount of air in the air/fuel mixture which the engine burns.

When you're starting a cold engine

- move the choke control to 'on'
- start the engine
- gradually move the choke control to 'off' as the engine warms up.

Failure to return the choke to 'off' could cause the engine to run faster than normal. This could make it difficult to control the motorcycle, especially when slowing down. In addition it could cause excessive wear to the engine and increased fuel consumption.

Familiarise yourself with the layout of the hand controls so that you can use them in the dark and while wearing thick gloves

Right handlebar controls

Engine cut-out switch

This is to stop the engine in an emergency.

When stopping the engine normally, use the ignition switch. You're less likely to leave your keys in the ignition when leaving your motorcycle. However, you should occasionally check that it operates correctly.

Electric starter

This is fitted as well as, or in place of, the kick starter.

Use - You should

- check the cut-out switch is on
- switch the ignition on
- make sure that the gear selector is in neutral
- press the starter button.

The throttle and front brake are the two main controls on the right handlebar

Light switch

On many new models dipped beam is automatically turned on when the ignition is turned on or the engine is started. With this arrangement there is no light switch. Parking lights are switched on by moving the ignition key to a 'Park' position.

On motorcycles not fitted with this feature the light switch is found on the right handlebar and is either a headlamp on/off switch or a three-position switch letting you select headlights, parking lights and off.

Front brake lever

Applies the brake to the front wheel (see page 59).

To apply the front brake squeeze the lever toward you. Use all the fingers on your right hand for maximum control and stopping power. The harder you squeeze, the harder you brake. To release the brake, release the lever.

Throttle

The throttle controls the engine speed. It increases or decreases the amount of fuel delivered to the engine. To speed up the engine twist the throttle towards you. To slow down the engine twist the grip away from you. Most throttles will spring back to a closed position when released. In this position the engine should run at 'idle' or 'tick over' speed.

Mirrors

Fitted to both right and left handlebars, or sometimes on the fairing.

Mirrors should be adjusted to give you the best view of the road behind. However, your elbows may obscure the view behind. If they do, try fitting mirrors with longer stems.

There are two types of mirror available

* **flat mirrors** - These don't distort the picture of the road behind. This makes it easier for you to judge the speed and distance of traffic behind you

* **convex mirrors** - These are slightly curved and give a wider field of vision. This makes it more difficult to judge the speed and distance of traffic behind you.

Foot controls

Gear selector

Gears enable you to match engine power to road speed. Low gears allow the engine power to be used at lower road speeds. Use these when you're moving off, going uphill or accelerating. High gears allow the same engine power to be used at higher road speeds.

Changing smoothly through the gears is a skill that improves with practice.

Position - The gear selector is usually on the left side of the motorcycle. It's just in front of the footrest.

Some mopeds and scooters have a twist-grip gear change on the left handlebar.

Neutral - The neutral position is when no gear is engaged. Most motorcycles have a green warning lamp to show when the gears are in neutral.

To select gears - On motorcycles the gears are selected by lifting or pushing down the gear lever with your foot. The positions and number of gears vary with the make and model of motorcycle.

The gear lever is usually on the left but on older motorcycles it is often on the right or even hand operated on some early vintage models

The green neutral lamp glows to indicate that the gears are in neutral

Thick-soled riding boots can affect the feel of the rear brake. You could find yourself braking harder than you intended

Rear brake pedal

This applies the brake to the rear wheel unless part of the linked braking system (see page 59).

Position - This pedal is usually on the right side of the motorcycle, just in front of the footrest. Some automatic motorcycles have the rear brake lever on the left handlebar.

Use - To apply the brake, press the pedal with your foot. To release the brake, release the pedal.

Kick-start lever

Position - Usually found on the right side of the motorcycle, near the footrest.

Use - You should

- make sure that the cut-out switch is on
- switch on the ignition
- put the gear selector in neutral and check that the neutral lamp glows
- fold out the kick-start lever (you may need to fold the footrest out of the way)
- tread down sharply on the lever. Repeat this until the engine starts.

Anti-lock braking systems

Anti-lock braking systems

Anti-lock braking systems (ABS) are designed to prevent wheel lock caused by excessive braking. This can enable the rider to achieve maximum braking when travelling in a straight line.

ABS cannot increase tyre grip or prevent skids where other factors are at work such as when cornering.

Wheel speed sensors detect when a wheel is beginning to lock. The system releases the braking pressure just enough to prevent wheel lock.

The sensor monitors wheel movement hundreds of times per second and will keep the wheel at the point of lock-up. This will happen for as long as the rider continues to brake hard enough to activate the system or until the motorcycle is stopped.

You should refer to the owner's handbook for details of the manufacturer's recommended method of use.

ABS cannot overcome the laws of physics. It will still be possible to skid because poor riding has failed to take account of the road conditions. ABS is a safety aid designed to enhance your skills, NOT replace them.

ABS warning lamp

Anti-lock braking systems will have a warning lamp. Generally it will light up when you turn on the ignition and may not go out until the motorcycle is travelling at 5-10 mph.

Read your owner's manual to find out how the system is designed to operate on your motorcycle.

Traction control and Linked braking systems

Traction control systems

Traction control systems (TCS) help prevent wheelspin when accelerating. This is most likely to occur on slippery surfaces. A sensor detects the rear wheel starting to spin and the system adjusts the power driving the rear wheel so that grip is maintained.

A warning lamp may glow to let you know when TCS is in operation.

TCS may also be activated by riding over a sudden change in road level - such as a hump backed bridge.

While TCS enables a rider to make maximum use of the tyres' grip during acceleration, it cannot prevent loss of grip caused by cornering too fast or failing to take account of road and weather conditions.

Linked braking systems

Some motorcycles have a linked braking system where use of one brake control activates front and rear brakes.

If your motorcycle has a linked brake system fitted refer to your owner's manual for the manufacturer's recommendations on their use. However, full braking effectiveness will be achieved by applying both brakes together.

section **six**

STARTING TO RIDE

This section covers

- Getting started
- Stands
- Mounting and dismounting
- Starting the engine
- Moving off
- Using the brakes
- Stopping safely
- Emergency braking
- Using the gears
- Signalling
- Moving off at an angle
- Moving off uphill

Getting started

This part takes you through the basics of motorcycle handling and control. Before you ride on busy roads and in traffic, you must have full control of your motorcycle at all times, and this involves a good working knowledge of the various controls and being able to coordinate hand and foot controls together.

In addition you need to have

- an understanding of the rules of the road
- a respect for the needs of other road users
- a basic knowledge to enable you to check to make sure everything is working correctly and the machine is safe before setting out.

Starting to ride isn't just a matter of starting the engine and setting off. You should first of all check your motorcycle to make sure it's safe and ready for the road.

Everyday checks

Make a habit of checking daily that

- there are no oil, petrol or water leaks
- all lights (including indicators) are working; replace any dead bulbs immediately (it's a good idea to carry spare fuses and bulbs)
- the brakes are working; don't ride with faulty brakes. Also that the wheels and tyres show no sign of damage.

Periodic checks

These checks are both for safety and good vehicle maintenance.

Check and top up if necessary

- engine oil
- water level in the radiator or expansion tank of liquid cooled engines
- brake fluid level
- battery - top up with distilled water if necessary (some batteries are maintenance free and don't need topping up).

You should also check tyres and make sure they are legal; they must have the correct tread depth and be free of dangerous cuts and defects. Check also that they are at the right pressure.

Clean your machine regularly, this will help you to identify any leaks, loose items or developing mechanical problems.

How often? - How often you make the checks depends on how much you ride. Consult your owner's handbook. If you ride a lot, you may need to do these every day.

Basic maintenance - Further information about basic motorcycle maintenance can be found in Section 15 of this manual.

Regular servicing - Have your motorcycle serviced regularly. The owner's handbook will give the recommended periods.

Stands

When you park a motorcycle you use a stand to support it. Motorcycles have either a centre or side stand, and many models are fitted with both.

Side stand

The side stand is generally quicker and easier to use than the centre stand. It relies on the motorcycle leaning over onto the stand for stability.

Allow enough room for the stand to rest on the road without catching the kerb

Care must be taken to ensure that

- the surface is firm enough to prevent the side stand sinking and the motorcycle falling over
- the slope of the ground doesn't prevent the motorcycle leaning onto the stand. If the machine is too upright it will be unstable.

To put your motorcycle on the side stand

- apply the front brake and dismount to the left of the motorcycle
- with the machine upright push the stand fully down with your foot
- let the machine lean towards you until its weight is taken on the stand
- turn the handlebars to the left and gently release the front brake.

To take your motorcycle off the side stand

- position yourself on the left of the motorcycle and apply the front brake
- turn the handlebars straight whilst pushing the motorcycle upright
- move the stand to its 'up' position with your foot. Make sure it locks securely
- mount the machine from the left.

Most side stands can be operated when you are sitting astride the motorcycle. To put your motorcycle on the side stand using this method

- apply the front brake and support the machine with both feet down
- push the side stand fully down with your left foot
- carefully let the machine lean to the left until its weight is taken on the stand
- as you dismount to the left turn the handlebars to the left and gently release the front brake.

To take your motorcycle off the side stand

- apply the front brake and turn the handlebars slightly to the right whilst pushing the motorcycle upright
- mount the motorcycle from the left and support it upright with both feet down
- straighten the handlebars and move the stand to its 'up' position with your left foot. Make sure it locks securely.

Remember that stands are designed only to take the weight of the motorcycle.

If the stand isn't fully up it could dig into the road when you're cornering and cause an accident. Some manufacturers fit a safety inhibitor switch to the side stand. Dependent upon the manufacturer, this prevents

- the engine being started while the side stand is down
- the engine running while the side stand is down
- the engine running if you try to ride off with the side stand down.

If your motorcycle refuses to start or the engine cuts out when you select a gear it could be that it is fitted with such a safety feature.

Centre stand

The centre stand gives more stable support than the side stand. It also supports the motorcycle so that maintenance such as drive chain adjustment (where fitted) and wheel removal can be carried out.

The centre stand needs to be used on a firm, level surface for maximum stability.

Remember, if the stand isn't fully up it could dig into the road when you're cornering and cause an incident.

To put your motorcycle onto the centre stand

- position yourself on the left of the motorcycle, holding the left handlebar with the left hand
- push the stand down with your right foot (or left foot, if preferred) and hold the frame near the saddle with your right hand (some machines have a special handle)
- tread down on the stand and pull the machine backwards and upwards.

To take your motorcycle off the centre stand

- hold the left handlebar with your left hand. Hold the frame near the saddle with your right hand
- position yourself on the left of the motorcycle. Put your right foot (or left, if preferred) firmly on the centre stand
- keep the handlebars straight and rock the motorcycle forward. When it comes off the stand, apply the front brake and allow the stand to retract. Lean the motorcycle towards you slightly to keep control.

Mounting and dismounting

Before mounting or dismounting your motorcycle look behind to make sure it is safe. Always mount from the left, and dismount to the left, the side away from the traffic.

Before you get on or off apply the front brake to stop the motorcycle moving.

Practise mounting and dismounting with the motorcycle off its stand.

Balancing and wheeling your motorcycle

After you've practised mounting and dismounting, wheel the machine forward. Leaning the motorcycle towards you slightly makes it easier to balance.

Work the front brake with your right hand to control the speed.

Practise wheeling the machine in circles, both to the left and to the right. Keep practising until you're able to balance and control it fully.

Adjusting the controls

You can adjust the main motorcycle controls to suit your individual needs. If you can't use them comfortably and safely when you're riding, adjust the hand controls (such as front brake and clutch levers) and the foot controls (such as the footbrake and gear selector).

Riding position

When you're seated on a stationary motorcycle you should be able to

- place both feet on the ground
- use one foot to keep your balance and the other to work the foot controls.

The best posture - Sit in a natural position, as determined by the machine design. You should be able to reach all the controls comfortably.

Starting the engine

Some engines can require a knack to make them start. The following is a general guide, but you may need to modify it to suit your machine. To start the engine

- make sure that the gear selector is in neutral. The neutral lamp on the instrument panel will glow when the ignition is turned on. If no neutral lamp is fitted push your motorcycle forward to see if the rear wheel turns freely
- turn the fuel tap to 'on'
- if the engine is cold move the choke to 'on'
- make sure that the engine cut-out switch is in the 'on' position
- turn the ignition key to the 'on' position.

Your motorcycle is now ready to start. The next step depends on whether your machine has an electric starter or a kick starter.

Electric starter

Press the starter button. As the engine starts, release the starter button and open the throttle to give a fairly high engine speed. As the engine warms up move the choke to 'off'.

Kick starter

Fold out the kick-start lever. On some machines you'll have to fold the footrest up before you can use the kick starter. Place your instep on the lever and tread down sharply. Allow the kick-start lever to return to its upright position. Repeat this until the engine starts.

When the engine has started, fold the kick-start lever back to its resting position. Open the throttle to give a fairly high engine speed and, as the engine warms up, move the choke to 'off'.

Stopping the engine

This safe sequence applies to most motorcycles

- close the throttle fully
- make sure that you're in neutral
- switch the ignition key to 'off'. Take out the key in the 'lock' position if you're leaving your machine
- turn the fuel tap to 'off' (if fitted).

Moving off

To move off safely you have to think about other road users. Can you move off without endangering yourself or anyone else? To answer this question you need to have a good look around.

> **Remember,** never look down at the front wheel when riding - this can severely upset your balance.

To move off, follow these steps in order

- sit astride your machine
- apply the front brake and then start the engine
- squeeze in the clutch lever. Use all your fingers to get full control
- select first gear keeping the clutch lever held in
- put your left foot on the ground and shift the weight of the machine to that foot. Put your right foot on the footrest and then apply the rear brake.

Now look around over your right shoulder (unless you're on the right-hand side of the road) and then look ahead. You're looking to make sure that there's no traffic approaching from behind and the way ahead is clear so that you're safe to move off.

Look out for pedestrians and cyclists - they're harder to see than cars. You should signal if it will help any other road user.

It's very important that you look around before moving off, even if you have mirrors fitted. Looking around will allow you to

- judge accurately how far away any traffic may be, and how fast it's travelling
- see if there's anything in the blind area on your right. The blind area is the area behind and to your right which isn't covered by mirrors (see Section 9 on 'Bends and junctions').

You can now release the front brake and work the throttle.

Clutch control

Release the clutch lever smoothly, until you feel the engine trying to move the machine. This is called the 'biting point'. You must be able to find the biting point easily when releasing the clutch lever. This skill will develop with practice. Open the throttle enough to keep the engine running smoothly.

Gradually release the clutch lever and at the same time open the throttle smoothly. As you move off release the rear brake and bring your left foot up onto the footrest.

Smooth clutch control is essential to good riding. It's also one of the most difficult skills for the novice to acquire.

Using the brakes

Many motorcycle riders are, quite wrongly, afraid to use the front brake. This is often as a result of what they were taught as cyclists. On a motorcycle

- you must normally use both brakes
- the front brake is the more powerful of the two brakes and the most important when stopping a motorcycle.

To stop most effectively

In good road and weather conditions

- apply the front brake just before you apply the rear brake
- apply greater pressure to the front brake.

Applying greater pressure to the front brake gives the best stopping power in good conditions because

- the combined weight of the machine and rider is thrown forward
- the front tyre is pressed more firmly on the road, giving a better grip.

In wet or slippery conditions you need to apply a more equal pressure to both front and rear brakes.

Using one brake only

You'll take much longer to stop by using one brake only. But at very low speeds (walking pace) using only the rear brake gives smoother control.

Coordinating both front and rear brakes correctly is an essential part of riding a motorcycle

When to brake

Always look and plan well ahead to avoid having to brake sharply. A gradual increase of pressure on the brakes is better than late, harsh braking.

Follow these rules

- brake when your machine is upright and moving in a straight line
- brake in good time
- adjust the pressure on the brakes according to the road surface and weather conditions.

Where to brake

Where you brake is very important. The best time to brake is when you're travelling upright in a straight line.

Braking on a bend - A good rider will plan well ahead to avoid braking on a bend.

On a bend the combined weight of motorcycle and rider is thrown outwards. To balance this the rider leans inwards.

If you brake on a bend

- the weight will be thrown outwards even more
- the motorcycle and rider may become unstable
- the tyres may lose their grip on the road surface.

If you must brake on a bend

- avoid using the front brake. Rely on the rear brake and engine braking to slow you down. If you must use the front brake, be very gentle. There's a risk of the front tyre losing its grip and sliding sideways
- try to bring your motorcycle upright and brake normally, provided you can do so safely.

Stopping safely

To stop safely you need to make sure that you don't endanger any other road users. You should

- use your mirrors and look over your right shoulder, if necessary, to check for traffic behind you
- signal if it will help other road users. People in front may benefit from a signal just as much as people behind.

Stopping

The following sequence will apply to most motorcycles

- roll off the throttle
- apply both brakes smoothly
- just before the motorcycle stops gently ease off the front brake and pull in the clutch lever to avoid stalling the engine
- as the machine comes to rest, put your left foot on the ground to support the weight.

When the machine has stopped

- apply the front brake
- release the rear brake and support the motorcycle with your right foot.

With the clutch lever still pulled in

- use your left foot to move the gear selector to neutral
- release the clutch lever
- place both feet on the ground.

Disengaging the clutch prevents the engine stalling when the motorcycle stops

Disengaging the clutch

When stopping from very low speeds pull in the clutch lever just before or just as you brake.

When stopping from higher speeds always brake first, then pull in the clutch lever just before you stop.

Some situations are unpredictable and you will need to respond quickly and with full control

Emergency braking

If you plan ahead you should seldom need to brake violently or stop suddenly. Nevertheless, emergencies do arise and you must be able to stop safely and quickly.

Maximum braking

- shut the throttle
- use the front brake just before the rear
- brake progressively (increase pressure steadily)
- apply the right amount of braking effort to each wheel. This will depend on the road surface and weather conditions.

Braking in an emergency

- keep your motorcycle upright
- apply maximum effort without locking the wheels. This is achieved by progressively increasing braking pressure. Don't use the brakes violently – this may cause you to skid (see pg 112 for more information about skidding)
- pull in the clutch just before you stop.

Signalling when you brake - Don't try to give an arm signal when you brake in an emergency because

- you'll need both hands on the handlebars
- your stop lamp will warn traffic behind that you are braking.

Using the gears

To change up or down through the gears you need to be able to co-ordinate the clutch, throttle and gear selector.

Changing up

Change gear when you've reached the appropriate speed for the next gear. To change gear you should

- simultaneously close the throttle and pull in the clutch lever
- select the next higher gear by lifting the gear selector with the toe of your boot. Allow the selector to return to its normal position after each change
- release the clutch lever smoothly and open the throttle at the same time
- repeat the sequence for each upward gear change.

Always travel in the highest suitable gear - you'll save fuel and spare your engine.

Changing down

Simultaneously close the throttle and pull in the clutch lever. Select the next lower gear by pushing down the gear selector with the toe of your boot. Allow the selector to return to its normal position after each gear change. At the same time, release the clutch lever smoothly and open the throttle as necessary.

When to change

Experience will tell you when to change gear. You'll be able to hear from the engine sound when a gear change is needed. Never let the engine

- race when you could change to a higher gear
- labour when you could change to a lower gear.

How many gears does a motorcycle have?

The number of gears on a motocycle varies with the make and model.

Most modern motorcycles have five or six gears while some smaller machines have four.

Can I miss out a gear?

The gears on a motorcycle have to be changed sequentially. This means you have to change to the next higher or lower gear in turn. It is possible to change to the next gear and, without releasing the clutch, immediately change again until you have selected the gear you require and then release the clutch.

Signalling

You need to give signals to help other road users know what you intend to do.

Road users include

- drivers of following and oncoming vehicles
- cyclists
- pedestrians
- traffic controllers
- police directing traffic.

Always signal clearly and in good time. Give only correct signals, as shown.

Arm signals

Arm signals are very effective in daylight especially when you're wearing bright or fluorescent clothing.

Giving an arm signal means that you have reduced steering control, if only briefly. Spend some time practising controlling your motorcycle while giving arm signals.

Practise

- with one hand and then with the other
- before you ride on the road.

Give arm signals in good time. Don't try to keep up the signal all the way through a turn. You'll need both hands on the handlebars to make any turn safely.

Arm signals at speed - When travelling at speed on the open road, arm signals can upset your stability. At speed it's safer to rely on your direction indicators, if fitted.

Arm signals at pedestrian crossings - When slowing down or stopping at a pedestrian crossing consider using an arm signal. This tells traffic behind you, approaching traffic and waiting pedestrians that you're slowing down.

Arm signals aren't a substitute for faulty direction indicators. The law requires that if direction indicators are fitted they must work.

Remember, approaching traffic and pedestrians can't see your brake lights.

Direction indicator signals

Indicator lamps are close together on a motorcycle and can be difficult to see. On some smaller machines the direction indicators don't show up very well in bright sunlight. You should

- consider giving an arm signal if you think your direction indicators may be difficult to see

- position yourself correctly and in good time for the manoeuvre you intend to perform.

Other types of signals

Stop lamps - Stop lamps come on when you apply the brakes. On a modern motorcycle the stop lamps are activated by the rear brake pedal and the front brake lever.

The stop lamps warn traffic behind you that you're braking. Help other road users by

- braking in good time
- slowing down gradually
- signalling in good time. Give an arm signal if necessary.

Flashing headlamps - You should only flash your headlamp as an alternative to the horn to warn others that you're there. Assume that other drivers mean the same. Don't flash your headlamp at anyone to go ahead or turn.

If someone flashes their headlamps at you make sure that you understand what they mean and it's you they're signalling to.

Never assume it's a signal to proceed.

Horn - Sound the horn only if you think someone may not have seen you or to warn other road users of your presence, for example at blind bends or junctions.

Sounding the horn doesn't give you the right of way. Always be prepared to stop.

You must not sound your horn

- between 11.30 pm and 7 am in a built-up area
- when your motorcycle is stationary, unless a moving vehicle poses a danger.

Never use your horn as a rebuke or to attract attention.

On high-speed roads drivers may not be able to hear your horn. In daylight, riding with your dipped headlamp on, can help you to be seen.

Whether using indicators, arm signals, headlamps or horn, always think about your signal.

- Is it necessary?
- Is it helpful?
- Is it misleading?

When you do signal, do so in good time, clearly and correctly.

Leave other road users in no doubt about your intentions. Giving signals properly is an important part of safe motorcycling.

Timing of signals

Whether you're giving arm signals or using direction indicators

- give your signal early enough to allow other road users to see and act on it
- don't give a signal so early that its meaning could mislead.

Conflicting signals

A signal must have one clear meaning. For example, signalling right to pass a parked vehicle might mislead. Other traffic may think that you intend to turn right or to pull over on the right. Avoid giving signals which could have two meanings.

Cancelling signals - Very few motorcycles have self-cancelling indicators. It's very important that you cancel a signal when you've completed the manoeuvre. Failure to cancel a signal could mislead another road user and cause an accident.

Sometimes a hand signal is necessary to reinforce a direction indicator such as here.
The indicator signal alone may be viewed as an intention to move around the obstruction
when the intention is to turn right

Before moving off it's essential that you look into the areas that are not visible in your mirrors

Moving off at an angle

When moving off at an angle – for instance, around a parked car – use the same procedure as for 'Moving off' covered earlier in this chapter.

Just before you move off ask yourself

- at what angle should I move out?
- how far will this take me into the road?

Your decision will depend on

- how close you are to the vehicle or object in front
- the width of the vehicle or object
- oncoming traffic.

Check all round for other vehicles and signal if necessary.

- Give yourself time to steer around the vehicle or object.
- Tight clutch and steering control are needed as you move off. Release the clutch completely as you clear the obstruction.
- Allow room for someone to open a door, if you're moving off around a vehicle.
- Be ready to brake – a pedestrian might step out from the other side of the vehicle or object.

Moving off uphill

Use the same procedure as for moving off straight ahead covered under 'Moving off' earlier in this chapter.

> **Remember,** allow a safe gap in any traffic because your motorcycle may be slower pulling away and building up speed.

Be aware that

- your motorcycle will tend to roll back. To avoid this, you must use the throttle, clutch and brakes together
- you may need to use more throttle when moving off uphill than you would when moving off on the level.

The motorcycle will stall if

- you hold the rear brake on too long
- you release the clutch too quickly
- you don't use enough throttle.

When you've mastered the technique then practise moving off uphill without rolling backwards, from behind a parked vehicle.

section **seven**
TRAFFIC SIGNS

This section covers

- The purpose of traffic signs
- Signs giving warning
- Signs giving orders
- Signs which give directions and other information
- Road markings
- Traffic lights
- Traffic calming
- Level crossings

The purpose of traffic signs

Signs are an essential part of any traffic system.

They tell you about the rules you must obey and warn you about the hazards you can meet on the road ahead.

Signs can be in the form of words or symbols on panels, road markings, beacons, bollards or traffic lights.

This section deals with the various types of traffic signs and their meaning.

To do its job, a sign must give its message clearly and early enough for you to

- see it
- understand it
- act safely on it.

Symbols

Symbols are used as much as possible because they're more easily recognised and understood. Many of them are standard symbols, particularly throughout Europe.

What are the basic rules of traffic signs?

You'll recognise traffic signs easier if you understand what the shapes and colours mean.

Rectangular signs - These inform and give directions.

Circular signs - These give orders. Blue circles tell you what you must do while signs with red rings tell you what you must not do.

Triangular signs - These warn you of something, such as a junction.

Road markings - These inform, give directions and give orders.

Other shapes - There are a few exceptions to these rules to give greater prominence to some signs.

Signs giving warning

Usually a red triangle pointing upwards, with a symbol or words on a white background.

These warn you of a hazard you might not otherwise be able to recognise in time, for example a bend, hill or hump-back bridge.

The sign will make clear what the hazard is. You must decide what to do about it.

Examples of warning signs

Narrowing roads - These tell you which side the road is narrowing from (sometimes both sides), and should warn you against overtaking until you have had a chance to assess the hazard.

Children and schools - The warning here is: watch out for children dashing out into the road, especially during school arrival and leaving times. Look out for school crossing patrols.

Low bridge sign - Even if your vehicle is low, watch out. An oncoming vehicle might have to use the centre of the road to make use of any extra headroom there.

Junctions - These tell you what type of junction is ahead: T-junction, crossroads, roundabout, staggered junction and so on. The priority through the junction is indicated by the broader line.

Sharp change of direction chevrons - These may be used where the road changes direction sharply enough to create a hazard or to reinforce a bend warning sign where stronger emphasis is needed.

Other hazards - If there's no special sign for a particular hazard, a general hazard warning sign is used: a red triangle with an exclamation mark on a white background. It will have a plate underneath telling you what the hazard is, e.g., hidden dip.

Signs giving orders

Signs which give orders can be

- mandatory signs; these tell you what you must do
- prohibitory signs; these tell you what you must not do.

Mandatory signs

Mostly circular signs with white symbols and borders on a blue background. For example mini roundabout, keep left and turn left. In addition

- Stop Children sign (lollipop) carried by school crossing patrols. This is circular with black lettering on a yellow background
- Stop in white on a red background, often manually controlled at roadworks
- Stop and Give Way signs appear at junctions and are very important for everyone's guidance and safety.

Stop signs

These are octagonal, with white lettering on a red background.

Usually at a junction with a limited zone of vision. Always accompanied by a stop line marked on the road. The line tells you how far forward you should go before stopping at the position from which you look, assess and decide if it is safe to proceed (PSL).

At a Stop sign - You must

- stop (even if you can see the road is clear)
- wait until you can enter the major road without causing other drivers to change speed or direction.

Give Way signs

These consist of a red triangle pointing downwards and black lettering on a white background.

They are always accompanied by road markings. However some junctions only have the Give Way lines. This is usually where there's relatively little traffic.

Give Way signs and/or road markings show you that traffic on the road you want to enter has priority.

The double broken lines across the road show you where to stop and wait, if necessary.

At a Give Way sign you must

- give way to traffic already on the major road
- delay entering the major road until you can do so without causing any traffic already on the major road to change speed or direction.

Prohibitory signs

These tell you what you must not do. They are easy to recognise by their circular shape and red border. The message is given by symbols, words or figures, or a combination of these.

Exceptions include a No Entry sign (circular with white border and red background) or a Bus Lane sign.

Speed limit signs

A red circle with a number on a white background shows the speed limit.

A white disc with a black diagonal line cancels the previous speed limit, but you must not exceed the national speed limit for the type of road you're on.

Repeater signs are a small form of the original speed limit sign which are fitted to lamp-posts to remind you of the speed limit.

Where there are lamp-posts, you should assume that the 30 mph speed limit normally applies, unless there are repeater signs showing a different speed limit.

Signs which give directions and other information

These help you find and follow the road you want. They can also direct you to the nearest railway station, car park, or other facility or attraction.

The colours of these signs vary with the type of road.

For example

- motorways – blue with white letters and border
- primary routes, except motorways – green with white letters and border, route numbers shown in yellow
- other routes – white with black letters and black or blue border.

All these roads may also display tourist signs, which are brown with white letters and border.

Types of signs giving directions on primary routes

Advance direction signs - You will see these before you reach the junction. They enable you to decide which direction to take and to prepare yourself.

Direction signs at the junction - These show you the way to take as you reach the junction.

Route confirmatory signs - Positioned after the junction, these confirm which road you're on.

These signs also tell you distances and places on your route. If the route number is in brackets, it means that the road leads to that route.

Information signs - These tell you where to find parking places, telephones, camping sites, and about no through roads, etc.

Road markings

Markings on the road give information, orders or warnings. They can be used with signs on posts or on their own.

Their advantages are

- they can often be seen when other signs are hidden by traffic
- they can give a continuing message as you travel along the road.

As a general rule, the more paint, the more important the message.

Lines across the road

Give Way lines - Double broken white lines across your half of the road show that traffic on the road you want to enter has priority.

The lines show where you should stop, if necessary, to take your final look. These may also be found on a roundabout where traffic on the roundabout is required to give way to those joining.

A single broken line is normally found at the entrance to a roundabout. This tells you that traffic coming from your immediate right has priority and you must give way.

Single Stop lines - A single continuous line across your half of the road shows where you must stop

- at junctions with Stop signs
- at junctions controlled by police or traffic lights
- at level crossings
- at swing bridges or ferries.

Lines along the road

Double white lines - The most important of these are double white lines and they have rules for

- overtaking
- parking.

Overtaking - When the line nearest you is continuous, you must not cross or straddle it except when it is safe and you want to

- enter or leave a side road or entrance on the opposite side of the road
- pass a stationary vehicle
- pass a road maintenance vehicle, pedal cycle or horse moving at 10 mph or less.

If there's a broken white line on your side and a continuous white line on the other, you may cross both lines to overtake. Make sure you can complete the manoeuvre before reaching a solid line on your side.

Arrows on the road often warn that there's a double white line coming up. Don't begin to overtake when you see them.

Parking - On a road marked with double white lines you must not stop or park, even if one of the lines is broken. You may, however, stop for a moment to pick up or drop off passengers.

Hatch markings - There are dangerous areas where it is necessary to separate the streams of traffic completely, such as a sharp bend or hump, or where traffic turning right needs protection. These areas are painted with white chevrons or diagonal stripes. Remember

- where the boundary line is solid, do not enter except in an emergency
- where the boundary line is broken, you should not ride on the markings unless you can see that it is safe to do so.

Single broken lines - Watch out for places where the single broken line down the centre of the road gets longer. This shows a hazard ahead.

Lane dividers - Short broken white lines are used on wide carriageways to divide them into lanes. You should keep between them unless you are overtaking or turning right.

Lanes for specific types of vehicle

Bus and cycle lanes are shown by signs and road markings. In some one-way streets these vehicles are permitted to travel against the normal flow of traffic. These are known as contraflow lanes.

Bus lanes - Only vehicles shown on the sign may use the lane during the times of operation which are also shown on the sign. Outside those periods all vehicles can use the bus lane.

Where there are no times shown, the bus lane is in operation for 24 hours a day. Don't use bus lanes when they are in operation unless motorcycles are shown on the sign as permitted vehicles.

Cycle lanes - Don't ride or park in a cycle lane marked by a solid white line during the times of operation shown on the signs.

If the cycle lane is marked by a broken line, don't ride or park in it unless it is unavoidable. If you park in a cycle lane at any time you can make it very dangerous for any cyclist who is using that lane.

Reflective studs

These are

- red on the left-hand side of the road
- white on the lane or centre-of-road lines
- amber on the right-hand edge of the carriageway on dual carriageways and motorways
- green between the carriageway and lay-bys, side roads and slip roads.

At road works, fluorescent green/yellow studs may be used to help identify the lanes in operation.

Box junction markings

Yellow criss-cross lines mark a box junction. Their purpose is to keep the junction clear by preventing traffic from stopping in the path of crossing traffic.

You must not enter a box junction unless your exit road is clear. But you can enter the box when you want to turn right and you're only prevented from doing so by oncoming traffic.

If there's a vehicle already on the junction waiting to turn right, you're free to enter behind it and wait to turn right – providing that you won't block any oncoming traffic wanting to turn right.

If there are a number of vehicles waiting to turn, it's unlikely you'll be able to proceed before the traffic signals change.

Reflective studs can be of the traditional cats eye type as here, or one piece plastic blocks

Words on the road can be obscured by queuing vehicles and this can make congestion worse. Leaving room between yourself and the vehicle in front should help you to see such instructions in good time

Words on the road

Words on the road surface usually have a clear meaning such as Stop, Slow, Keep Clear.

When they show a part of the road is reserved for certain vehicles, for example, buses, taxis or ambulances, don't ride there.

Schools

Yellow zigzags are often marked on the road outside schools, along with the words School – keep clear. Do not stop or park there.

The markings are to make sure that

- drivers passing and
- children crossing

have a clear, unrestricted view of the crossing area.

Destination markings

Near a busy junction, lanes sometimes have destination markings or road numbers on the road surface. These enable you to get into the correct lane early, even if advance direction road signs are obscured.

Speed reduction lines

Raised yellow lines may be painted across the carriageway at the approach to

- roundabouts
- reduced speed limits when entering a village
- particular hazards.

The purpose of these lines is to make you aware of your speed after a period of travel at higher speeds. Reduce your speed in good time.

Lane arrows

These tell you which lane to take for the direction you want.

Where the road is wide enough, you may find one arrow pointing in each direction

- left in the left-hand lane
- straight ahead in the centre lane
- right in the right-hand lane.

Some arrows might be combined, depending on how busy the junction is. If the road is only wide enough for two lanes, arrows might have two directions combined

- straight ahead and left in the left-hand lane
- straight ahead and right in the right-hand lane.

Arrows indicating left and right turns are placed well before a junction to help you get into the correct lane in good time. They don't indicate the exact point at which you should turn. It's especially important to remember this at right turns.

Traffic lights

Traffic lights have three lights which change in a set cycle

- red
- red and amber
- green
- amber
- red.

What the colours mean

- red – stop and wait at the Stop line
- red and amber – stop and wait. Don't go until green shows
- green – go if the way is clear
- amber – stop, unless you've already crossed the line or you're so close to it that pulling up might cause an accident.

Approaching green traffic lights

Approach traffic lights as you would any other junction. Keep your speed down.

Don't speed up to 'beat the lights'. Be ready to stop, especially if the lights have been green for some time.

Green filter arrow

A green arrow in a traffic light means you can filter in the direction the arrow is pointing, even if the main light is not showing green.

Don't enter this lane unless you want to go in the direction shown by the arrow.

When turning left or right at traffic lights take special care, and give way to pedestrians already crossing.

OSM/PSL routine

Use the Observation–Signal –Manoeuvre (OSM) and Position–Speed–Look (PSL) routines as you approach the lights. See page 138.

Pay attention to lane markings and get into the correct lane in good time. Be prepared to stop.

Advance Stop lines

At some traffic lights there are advance Stop lines to allow cyclists to position themselves ahead of other traffic.

Stop at the first white line. Do not encroach on the marked area, which is reserved for cyclists only. Allow the cyclists time and space to move off when the lights change to green.

In some areas there are bus advance areas, these should be treated in the same way as those provided for cyclists.

Special traffic lights

These are often used to control traffic where low-flying aircraft pass over the road, or at swing or lifting bridges, or other special sites such as fire stations.

They may either be

- normal traffic lights (red, amber and green) – follow the normal rules
- double red flashing lights, stop when the red lights are flashing.

If traffic lights fail

If the traffic lights fail, proceed with caution. Treat the situation as you would an unmarked junction and never assume priority.

If school crossing warning signals are flashing you should expect the crossing to be in use and should approach with care

School crossing warning

Two amber lights flashing alternately warn traffic of a school crossing point ahead at some busy locations.

Keep your speed down and proceed with great care.

Traffic calming

Traffic calming measures are used to encourage people to reduce speed more than they might otherwise do. They are used in particularly sensitive areas where it is considered that a reduction in speed would benefit the immediate community.

Various features can be provided to slow down the speed of traffic

- road humps
- road narrowings, central islands and chicanes
- mini roundabouts.

20 mph zones

Some traffic-calmed areas are indicated only by a 20 mph speed limit sign.

At mini roundabouts you should avoid riding on the white paint as it can be slippery especially when it's wet

This speed limit sign, in addition to advising the maximum speed limit, also indicates that there may be traffic calming features within the signed zone and these may not be individually signed.

You should ride at a steady speed within the speed limit, and avoid frequent acceleration and deceleration within these areas.

Road humps

These may be round or flat topped humps laid across the carriageway. They may be used on roads where there is a speed limit of 30 mph or less.

In some areas the humps are in the form of 'cushions' which only cover part of the lane and are designed so that larger vehicles, especially buses, can straddle them.

If these are provided outside 20 mph zones, there will normally be

- warning signs at the beginning of the section of road where the hump or series of humps are installed
- triangle and edge line markings at each hump.

Road narrowings

Roads may be narrowed by the use of build outs on one or both sides of the road.

If these are provided outside 20 mph zones, there will normally be

- warning signs indicating which side of the road narrowing occurs
- Give Way road markings on one side of the road accompanied by signs advising priority for oncoming vehicles.

If these are on your side of the road, you must always give way to vehicles approaching from the other direction.

If priority is not given in either direction, then ensure you can pass through the narrowing without endangering vehicles approaching from the other direction. You should not accelerate as you approach the narrowing, but be prepared to slow down or give way to approaching traffic. Don't try to squeeze through at the same time as these vehicles.

Mini roundabouts

Mini roundabouts are often used as part of traffic-calming schemes to break up a long road into shorter sections and allow traffic to join from minor roads.

Methods of dealing with mini roundabouts are given on page 153.

Traffic calming is found in most larger towns and road narrowing build outs are a common feature

Level crossings

At a level crossing, the road crosses railway lines. Approach and cross with care. Never

- ride onto the crossing unless the road is clear on the other side
- ride over it 'nose to tail'
- stop on or just after the crossing
- park close to the crossing.

Most crossings have full or half barriers, some crossings have no gates or barriers.

Crossings with automatic barriers

Crossings with lights - A steady amber light followed by twin flashing red lights warn of an approaching train. An audible alarm to warn pedestrians will also sound once the lights show. You must obey the lights' signals.

Don't

- move onto the crossing after the lights show
- stop on the crossing if the amber light or audible alarm starts to operate – keep going if you're already on the crossing
- zigzag round half barriers.

If the train goes by and the red lights continue to flash, or the audible alarm changes tone, you must wait because another train is approaching.

Crossings without lights - At crossings with no lights, stop when the gates or barriers begin to close.

At an open crossing never ride across when the lights are showing; the train cannot stop for you

Open crossings

The sign in the shape of the cross shown in the picture above is used at all level crossings without either gates or barriers.

Crossings with lights - Automatic open level crossings have flashing road traffic signals and audible warnings similar to those on crossings with barriers.

Crossings without lights - At an open crossing with no gates, barriers, attendant or traffic signals, there will be a 'Give Way' sign.

Look both ways, listen and make sure there's no train coming before you cross.

User-operated crossings

These crossings are normally private and should be used by authorised users and invited guests only.

Crossings with signals - Some crossings with gates or barriers have Stop signs and small red and green lights. Do not cross when the red light is on because this means that a train is approaching. Cross only when the green light is on.

You should

- open the gates or barriers on both sides of the crossing
- check the green light is still on and cross promptly
- close the gates or barriers when you're clear of the crossing.

Crossings without signals - Some crossings have gates but no signals. At these crossings, stop, look both ways and listen and make sure that no train is approaching.

If there's a railway telephone you must contact the signal operator to make sure it's safe to cross.

Open the gates on both sides of the crossing and check again that no train is coming before crossing promptly.

Once you've cleared the crossing close both gates and, if there's a telephone inform the signal operator.

Always give way to trains – they can't stop easily.

Breakdowns

If your motorcycle breaks down on the crossing get yourself, any passenger and your motorcycle clear of the crossing immediately.

If you can't move your motorcycle immediately, get yourself and any passenger clear of the crossing. If there's a railway telephone, use it immediately to inform the signal operator then follow any instructions you're given.

If there's time before a train arrives, move your motorcycle clear of the crossing. However, if the alarm sounds, or the amber light comes on, get clear of the crossing at once – the train will not be able to stop.

Tram crossings (LRTs)

Look for traffic signs which show where trams cross the road. Treat them the same as normal railway crossings.

> **Remember,** modern trams are silent. Take extra care and look both ways before crossing.

Several large cities now have tram systems where the road is shared with the trams and traffic lights control places where trams cross the road

section **eight**
ON THE ROAD

This section covers

- Awareness and anticipation
- Mirrors
- Rear observation
- Road position
- Stopping distance
- The road surface
- Skidding
- Separation distance
- Overtaking
- Obstructions
- Pedestrian crossings
- Tunnels
- Parking

Awareness and anticipation

In any traffic situation there are some things that are obviously going to happen, as well as some things that might happen.

To anticipate is to take action when you expect something will or might happen.

You can anticipate what might happen by making early use of the available information on the road.

Ask yourself

- what am I likely to find?
- what are other road users trying to do?
- should I speed up or slow down?
- do I need to stop?

Changing conditions

Traffic conditions change constantly and you need to

- check and re-check what's going on around you
- be alert all the time to changes in conditions, and think ahead.

The degree to which you need to anticipate varies according to those conditions.

Difficult conditions

You'll find it more difficult to decide what might happen when

- the light or the weather is poor
- the traffic is heavy
- the route is unfamiliar.

Types of road

Similarly, types of road will affect how much you can anticipate.

It's easier in light traffic to anticipate what other drivers might do. It is more difficult on a busy single carriageway, dual carriageway or motorway, where their options are greater.

99

Riding ahead

Read the road ahead to anticipate what might happen.

You need to be alert and observant at all times.

Assess the movement of all other road users, including pedestrians, on the whole stretch of road you're travelling on.

Take in as much as possible of the road ahead, behind and to each side.

You should keep scanning the area in your view and

- be able to observe the middle distance and far distance as well as the area immediately in front
- glance frequently in the mirror to see what's happening in the area you've just passed.

Observation

If you're a new rider, you'll tend to give more of your attention to controlling the motorcycle.

Practise reading the road. You don't have to be riding to do this. You can do it as a passenger on a motorcycle or in a car or bus. Look out for

- other vehicles and pedestrians
- signals given by others
- road signs and markings
- the type and condition of the road surface
- movements of vehicles well ahead of you, as well as the one immediately in front
- side roads or hills ahead. The building line may show these
- buses signalling to move out from bus stops.

Clues

Look out for clues to help you to act safely and sensibly on what you see.

Watch smaller details in built-up areas where traffic conditions change rapidly. Observe other road users' actions and reactions.

Reflections in shop windows can often give important information where vision is restricted.

A pedestrian approaching a zebra crossing might step out into the road sooner than you think.

Take care approaching parked vehicles, especially if someone is in the driving seat.

Watch out for a driver stopping to set down or pick up a passenger. You may find they move off without warning or without checking in the mirrors or looking around.

When following a bus, watch for passengers standing up inside - the bus will probably stop shortly.

Observing is not just seeing - How much you can see depends on how well you can see.

Your eyesight can change without you being aware of it. Have regular eyesight checks.

Your ears can also warn of what's happening around you.

Remember, try to anticipate the actions of other road users.

At works entrances and schools you should expect an increase in pedestrians, cyclists and vehicles. Watch for vehicles picking up and setting down at school times – buses as well as cars.

Emergency vehicles

Look and listen for emergency vehicles such as fire engines, ambulances, police and other emergency services using blue, red or green flashing lights or sirens.

You should try to keep out of their way. Check where they are coming from - behind (mirrors), ahead or, more importantly, across your path.

Do not panic. Watch for the path of the emergency vehicle and take any action you can to try to help it get through. If necessary pull into the side of the road and stop, but do not endanger yourself or other road users.

Riding in busy areas

When riding in busy areas, you should be especially alert to all the possible hazards already mentioned.

You should also be particularly aware of your speed and always ride at a speed appropriate to the conditions.

The speed limit is the absolute maximum and does not always mean that it is safe for you to ride at that speed. For example, in a narrow residential street with cars parked on either side, you may need to reduce your speed considerably.

While you should make room for an emergency vehicle if you can, don't break the law to do so, for example by speeding or passing a red traffic light

Mirrors

Mirrors must be adjusted to give a clear view behind. They should be kept clean and smear-free.

When you're riding you might find that your elbows or shoulders obstruct the view behind. To overcome this, adjust your mirrors to the best position. If this problem remains you can solve it by extending the mirrors with longer stems.

If your mirrors vibrate your view will be distorted. Your motorcycle dealer may be able to offer advice on how to reduce the vibration.

Using the mirrors

Glancing regularly into your mirrors will keep you up to date with the traffic situation behind.

Use your mirrors before

- signalling
- changing direction
- overtaking
- changing lanes
- slowing down or stopping.

Use your mirrors together with looking behind, where necessary.

Just looking isn't enough!

Whether you look in your mirrors or over your shoulder

- you must act on what you see
- think about how your actions will affect traffic behind you.

Rear observation

Rear observation refers to a combination of mirror checks and looking behind which ensures you're always fully aware of what's happening behind you.

Before you signal, change direction or change speed you must know how your actions will affect traffic behind you. You also have to know when traffic is likely to overtake or come alongside you.

Looking behind is important because not all motorcycles are fitted with mirrors, and mirrors don't always give a clear view behind, leaving significant blind spots. There will be times when you need to look around to see the full picture.

Looking behind also warns other drivers that you may be about to signal or alter course.

When to look behind

Use judgement in deciding when to look behind. Obviously when you're looking behind you're not looking ahead. This could be hazardous if, for example, you're close to the vehicle in front or if you're overtaking at speed. Equally there are situations when it is dangerous not to look behind, such as at a right turn into a minor road.

Take rear observation when you're about to change position or speed as you approach and negotiate a hazard. This might be before

- moving off
- turning left or right
- overtaking
- changing lanes
- slowing or stopping.

Warning - Looking over your shoulder too often or at the wrong moment can be hazardous. In the time you take to look behind, you

- lose touch with what's going on in front
- run the risk of veering off course.

At high speed or in congested moving traffic your attention needs to be focused ahead. In these situations time your rearward checks carefully.

Combine regular and sensible use of the mirrors with the 'lifesaver' check into the blind area before altering course.

The 'lifesaver' check

The 'lifesaver' is a last check over the shoulder into the blind spot to make sure nothing unexpected is happening before committing yourself to a manoeuvre.

If you're turning, use it to check the blind spot on the side you intend to turn. Use your judgement about when to use it - in congested urban situations a lifesaver check is normally essential, especially when turning right into a minor road, but during high speed overtaking, when you're certain what's happening behind, it's often safer to keep your eyes on what's happening ahead.

When checking your blind area make sure your steering and balance aren't affected while you're looking around

The blind area

The blind area is the area behind and to either side of you which isn't covered by mirrors. It's very important to check for traffic in this area before

- moving off
- changing direction
- changing lane.

Road position

As a general rule, keep to the centre of the lane. On a single carriageway (two-way traffic) that is halfway between the centre of the road and the left side.

Your position will depend on

- the width of the road
- the road surface
- your view ahead
- any obstructions.

Your position should allow you to

- be easily seen by traffic ahead, particularly vehicles emerging from junctions
- be seen in the mirror of any vehicle in front
- move over to the left to create more room for oncoming traffic that's passing stationary vehicles or other obstructions.

Keep clear of the gutter, where there are often potholes and loose grit.

Avoid riding in the centre of the road. You might

- obstruct overtaking traffic
- put yourself in danger from oncoming traffic
- encourage traffic behind you to overtake you on your left.

The correct position - You should always be in the correct position for the route you're going to take.

- Keep to the left if you're going straight ahead or turning left.
- Keep as close to the centre of the road as is safe when you're turning right.

Your position is important not only for safety, but also to allow the free flow of traffic. A badly positioned vehicle can hold up traffic in either direction.

One-way streets - Position according to whether you intend to go ahead, turn left, or turn right.

- To turn left, keep to the left-hand lane.
- To turn right, keep to the right-hand lane, provided there are no obstructions or parked vehicles on the right-hand side of the road you are in.
- To go ahead, be guided by the road markings. If there is no specific lane for ahead, select the most appropriate lane, normally the left, in good time.

Follow the road markings and get into the correct lane as soon as possible and stay in this lane. Watch for drivers who may change lane suddenly.

Traffic in one-way streets often flows freely. Watch out for vehicles coming past on either side of you.

Lane discipline

You should always follow lane markings, which are there for two reasons

- they make the best possible use of road space
- they guide the traffic.

Keeping to the lane markings is vital.

Position yourself in good time - If you find you're in the wrong lane and you don't have time to change lane safely, carry on in your lane and find another way back to your route.

Changing lanes - Position your vehicle according to your route. Always check behind and signal in good time before you change lanes, and

- never weave from lane to lane
- never change lanes at the last minute
- always stay in the middle of your lane until you need to change.

In heavy and slow moving traffic don't obstruct keep-clear markings. Watch out for these in congested, slow-moving traffic, especially at exits for emergency vehicles.

Allow for

- pedestrians crossing
- cyclists moving up the nearside
- large vehicles needing to straddle lanes before turning
- doors opening.

Riding ahead - Keep to the left-hand lane wherever possible. Don't use the right-hand lane just because you're travelling at speed.

On a carriageway with four or more lanes, don't use the lanes on the right unless signs or markings allow you to do so. Peak hour 'tidal flow' systems might permit or forbid use of these lanes, depending on the time of day.

Bus and cycle lanes - These are separate lanes shown by signs and road markings. Do not enter these lanes unless permitted by the signs.

Lane markings indicate the correct lane to use but ride defensively and remember that in queuing traffic the road markings will not be so easy to see

Approaching a road junction

Look well ahead for signs and markings.

If you have two lanes in your direction and

- you intend to turn left, stay in the left-hand lane
- you intend to go ahead, stay in the left-hand lane unless otherwise indicated
- you intend to turn right, move to the right-hand lane in good time.

Don't try to gain an advantage by using an incorrect lane. Trying to change back to the proper lane at, or near, the junction is a risky business.

If you have three lanes in your direction and you intend to

- turn left, stay in the left-hand lane
- go ahead, take the left-hand lane (unless there are left filter signs) or the middle lane, or be guided by road markings
- turn right, take the right-hand lane.

Slip road - Some junctions also have a slip road.

Get into the left-hand lane in good time before entering the slip road. You'll be able to use the slip road to slow down to turn left without holding up other traffic.

Stopping distance

It's important for you to know the stopping distance at all speeds. This is the distance your motorcycle travels

- from the moment you realise you must brake
- to the moment your machine stops.

Always ride so that you can stop safely within the distance you can see to be clear.

Stopping distance depends on

- how fast you're going
- whether you're travelling uphill, on the level or downhill
- the weather and the state of the road
- the condition of your brakes and tyres
- your ability, especially your reaction times.

Stopping distance divides into thinking distance and braking distance.

Thinking distance

'Thinking distance' is from the point where you see the hazard to the point where you start to brake.

This distance will vary from rider to rider and is dependent upon reaction time. Reaction times are affected by

- age
- physical and mental condition
- health
- time of day
- alcohol or drugs.

An alert and fit rider needs 0.75 of a second thinking time. That means that at 50 mph you'll travel about 15 metres (about 50 feet) before you begin to brake.

What are the usual stopping distances?

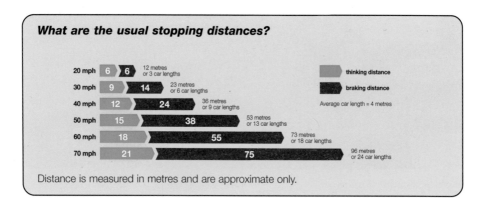

	thinking distance	braking distance
20 mph	6	6	12 metres or 3 car lengths
30 mph	9	14	23 metres or 6 car lengths
40 mph	12	24	36 metres or 9 car lengths
50 mph	15	38	53 metres or 13 car lengths
60 mph	18	55	73 metres or 18 car lengths
70 mph	21	75	96 metres or 24 car lengths

Average car length = 4 metres

Distance is measured in metres and are approximate only.

Braking distance

'Braking distance' is from the point where you begin to brake to the point where you stop.

Braking distance depends upon

- road conditions
- tyre condition
- brake efficiency
- suspension efficiency
- load. It takes longer to stop if you're carrying a passenger
- rider ability.

Most of all, braking distance varies with speed. At 30 mph your braking distance will be about 14 metres (about 45 feet) while at 70 mph that distance will increase to about 75 metres (about 245 feet).

That's just over double the speed but more than five times the braking distance.

Overall stopping distance

Your overall stopping distance also increases dramatically as you increase your road speed.

You may be surprised to find out how much your speed affects how far you will travel before stopping

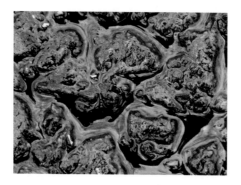 

The road surface

The state of the road surface is very important to motorcyclists. Only a small part of the motorcycle tyre makes contact with the road. Any change in the surface can therefore affect the stability of your motorcycle.

Be on the lookout for poor road surfaces. Beware of

- loose surfaces, such as chippings, gravel, mud and leaves
- potholes and uneven surfaces
- inspection covers, especially when wet
- oil patches and spilt fuel, especially at roundabouts, bus stops and filling stations
- tar banding around road repairs
- painted road markings

- rails set into the road for trams or light rapid transit (LRT) systems. These can affect your steering and present a hazard when braking
- any shiny road surface. At junctions, frequent braking and acceleration can polish the surface.

If you can safely avoid riding on slippery surfaces then do so. If you have to ride on a slippery surface slow down well in advance. Don't swerve suddenly to avoid a poor surface.

If you find yourself on a slippery surface check the traffic, then gradually slow down.

Section twelve, 'Riding in bad weather', contains information on the effects of weather on the road surface.

Skidding

A skid is when tyres

- lose their grip on the road surface
- veer off the steered course
- reduce the effect of the brakes (by sliding over the road surface).

Causes of skidding

Skidding can be caused by a number of things including

- heavy or uncoordinated braking, which locks one or both wheels
- excessive acceleration, causing the rear wheel to spin
- swerving (a sudden change of direction)
- leaning over too far when cornering, causing one or both tyres to lose grip.

A good rider tries to avoid skidding. The loss of control which can arise from a skid can be lethal.

Dealing with skids

Skids can happen suddenly. You need to know how to regain control when skidding occurs.

New road surfaces can be very slippery, even in dry conditions, for several days after being replaced

Excessive acceleration - If you've caused a skid by excessive acceleration

- the rear wheelspin can cause your machine to slide sideways. Steer in the direction that your machine is sliding
- ease off the throttle to regain control.

Braking - If you've caused a skid by braking

- release the brakes to let the wheels start turning again
- reapply the brakes as firmly as the conditions will permit.

Your natural instincts when dealing with a skid caused by excessive braking will be to brake even harder. You must learn to overcome such instincts if you're to regain control.

Tyre grip - If your motorcycle skids when cornering or changing direction

- steer into the skid. If the machine is sliding to the right, steer to the right. If the machine is sliding to the left, steer to the left

Remember, skid control is an emergency measure – it's no substitute for skid avoidance.

- keep your feet on the footrests. Putting your feet to the ground on a moving motorcycle could upset your balance.

113

Separation distance

How far must you keep from the vehicle in front? Ideally you should be no closer than the stopping distance that corresponds to your speed. In some traffic situations that may not be possible. The gap must never be less than your thinking distance, and much more if the road is wet or slippery.

In good conditions the two-second rule is a simple yet effective way to ensure you aren't too close to the vehicle in front

One method of judging separation distance is to allow 1 metre (just over 3 feet) for each mph of your speed. For example, at 45 mph leave a gap of 45 metres (about 150 feet).

A useful technique for judging 1 metre per mph is to use the 'two-second rule'.

The two-second rule

In good conditions an experienced rider needs to be at least two seconds behind the vehicle in front.

To measure this gap

- select a stationary object on the side of the road, for example a road sign
- as the vehicle in front passes the object say to yourself, 'Only a fool breaks the two-second rule'.

If you reach the object before you finish saying the sentence, you're too close.

In bad weather, at least double this gap between you and the vehicle in front.

Separation distance behind

When the vehicle behind is following too closely, slow down gradually. You need to increase the gap between you and the vehicle in front. This will give

- you more time to brake if necessary
- the following vehicle a better chance to overtake.

Overtaking

Don't overtake unless it's necessary. For example, don't rush to get past someone only to turn off shortly afterwards.

Ask yourself if it's really necessary. If you decide it is, you need to find a suitable place.

You must not overtake where to do so would cause you to break the law. Details are shown in *The Highway Code.*

In addition, some places are never suitable. For example, don't overtake

- if your view ahead is blocked
- if others might not be able to see you
- if there isn't enough room
- if the road narrows
- if you're approaching a junction
- if you're within the zigzag area of a pedestrian crossing
- if there's a no-overtaking sign
- if you have to cross a continuous central white line on your side of the road. The exception to this rule is when it's safe to pass an obstruction such as a road maintenance vehicle, a cyclist or a horse. They must be either stationary or travelling at less than 10 mph
- if there's dead-ground, that is a dip in the road which might conceal an oncoming vehicle.

Judging speed and distance

If you're travelling at 50 mph and an oncoming vehicle is travelling at the same speed, you're approaching each other at 100 mph or 45 metres (about 150 feet) per second. This can be difficult to judge accurately so give yourself plenty of time.

Take great care if you're travelling on a two-way three-lane road. An oncoming vehicle might pull out to overtake while you're overtaking. Wearing bright clothing and riding with your dipped headlamp on will help oncoming drivers to see you. Nevertheless, be aware of the hazard.

When you're following slower traffic and looking for the chance to overtake, keep a safe distance. Staying back will help you to see past the vehicle in front, and give you time to react to its signals.

Filtering

The small size of a motorcycle makes it possible to filter through slow or stationary queues of traffic. Filtering requires great care and can expose you to additional hazards.

You must comply with *The Highway Code* and when filtering you need to

- ride slowly and be prepared to stop
- watch for
  - vehicles suddenly changing lane
  - sudden opening of doors
  - pedestrians and cyclists
  - vehicles emerging or turning at junctions
  - road markings or studs which could upset your balance.
- be ready to brake and/or use the horn if you don't think you've been seen.

Remember, other road users may not be expecting a filtering motorcycle. Make yourself easy to see by wearing bright clothing and use your headlamp on dipped beam.

Before overtaking

Many danger spots are marked with double white lines along the road. Look out for arrows warning you to move over to the left as you are approaching these areas.

On three-lane roads, junction signs and hatch markings in the middle of the road are warnings not to overtake. Be ready to hold back in case traffic is waiting to turn right or slowing to turn left.

Watch the vehicle in front - Before overtaking, decide what the driver in front is likely to do by watching both them and the road ahead for a while. They might

- decide to overtake
- continue to drive at the speed of the vehicle ahead of them
- intend to turn off soon
- have seen something ahead which you haven't.

Vehicles turning right - Research has shown that most overtaking accidents are caused by the overtaking vehicle hitting a vehicle which is turning right. To avoid this type of accident you should

- consciously check the indicators of the vehicle you are about to overtake
- assume that a vehicle that is slowing down is about to turn.

Following through - Never automatically follow an overtaking vehicle without being able to see for yourself that the way is clear. The vehicle in front obscures your view and hides you from the view of oncoming traffic.

Always make your own decisions about overtaking based on

- what you see
- what you know.

Be patient. If in doubt, hold back.

Overtaking procedure

To overtake, use the OSM/PSL routine.

Observation - Take observation well ahead and behind.

Signal - Consider signalling.

Manoeuvre - Use the PSL routine:

Position - Check your position. Be near enough to the vehicle ahead to overtake smoothly when you're ready, but not so close that you can't get a good view of the road ahead.

Speed - Do you have enough speed and acceleration to overtake? Be fast enough to keep up with the vehicle in front and with enough reserve power to pass it briskly.

You might need to change down to get extra acceleration when you're ready to start overtaking.

Look - Look. Assess the whole situation

- the state of the road
- what the driver ahead is doing or might be about to do
- any hazards
- the speed and position of oncoming vehicles
- the speed difference between you and oncoming vehicles.

If you have any doubts, don't overtake.

Remember, when overtaking cyclists or horse riders give them plenty of room.

When you overtake you should

- consider a 'lifesaver' glance just before you move out
- overtake as quickly as you can and don't cut in front of the vehicle you've just passed
- cancel your signal when you've finished overtaking
- never automatically follow an overtaking vehicle. Your view of the road ahead may be obstructed.

If you can't see clearly ahead, wait. Never attempt to overtake just before turning left.

Overtaking on the left

You should never overtake on the left unless

- the vehicle in front is signalling an intention to turn right, and you can safely overtake on the left
- traffic is moving slowly in queues, and vehicles in the lane on your right are moving more slowly than you are.

Take care if there is a road to the left. Oncoming traffic turning right into it may be hidden by the vehicle you're overtaking.

Passing on the left - In addition you can go past on the inside of slower traffic when

- you're in a one-way street (but not a dual carriageway) where vehicles are allowed to pass on either side
- you're in the correct lane to turn left at a junction.

Overtaking on dual carriageways

Don't overtake unless you're sure that you can do so safely. Use the appropriate parts of the OSM/PSL routine.

Observation - Use your mirrors. Take rear observation if necessary.

Position - Position yourself so that you can see well ahead past the vehicle in front.

Speed - Make sure that you have enough reserve speed to overtake.

Look - Look ahead to make sure that the lane you want to join is clear.

Remember, if you're travelling at high speed it's safer to combine regular, sensible use of the mirrors with the 'lifesaver' glance before changing course.

If you're satisfied that it's safe to overtake, use OSM again.

Manoeuvre - Manoeuvre. Don't forget the 'lifesaver' glance into the blind area before you change course. Overtake quickly and decisively. Cancel your signal promptly and return to the left lane only when you're clear of the vehicle you've overtaken. Don't cut in.

Lane discipline - Use the left-hand lane unless the amount of slow-moving traffic would cause you to be constantly changing lanes. Don't weave from lane to lane.

Where there are three lanes, don't ride in the middle lane if the left lane is clear. Always return to the left lane when you've finished overtaking.

Obstructions

The secret of dealing with any obstruction lies in looking and planning well ahead, combined with early and sensible use of the OSM/PSL routine.

The decision to wait or go on will depend on

- the type and width of road
- whether the obstruction is on your side of the road or the other side of the road or on both sides of the road
- whether there is approaching traffic
- the room available.

As a general rule, if the obstruction is on your side of the road, approaching traffic will have priority.

Don't assume that you have priority if the obstruction is on the other side of the road. Always be prepared to give way.

Procedure

Look well ahead to identify the obstruction in good time before using the OSM/PSL routine.

Observation - Use your mirrors. Take rear observation if necessary.

Signal - Signal if necessary.

If you have to stop and wait, keep well back from the obstruction in a position that not only keeps your zone of vision open, but also doesn't impede the approaching traffic

Position - Decide on your position. Avoid keeping too far in to the left so that you have to change direction at the last minute; a gradual change of course is required.

Speed - Adjust your speed as necessary. This will depend on the situation, but aim to regulate your speed to take a smooth and steady course without stopping.

Look - Finally, look and assess the situation before you decide whether it's necessary to wait or safe to proceed.

If you need to pass an obstruction, make sure you can see it's safe and don't blindly follow the vehicle in front

Obstructions on hills - These need special care. If travelling downhill allow extra time and space for braking.

If you're travelling downhill and the obstruction is on the other side of the road, don't take your priority for granted. If it's safe, be prepared to let other traffic coming uphill, especially heavy vehicles, have a clear run. Your consideration will be appreciated.

Defensive riding - Don't follow through behind the vehicle in front without being able to see for yourself that the way is clear ahead.

Keep a safe distance from the obstruction and the approaching traffic. Where space is limited, reduce speed and take extra care. The less space that is available, the lower the speed needs to be.

Pedestrian crossings

People on foot have certain rights of way at pedestrian crossings, but are safe only if everyone sticks to the rules and does the right thing.

Types of crossing

There are various types of pedestrian crossings

Zebra crossings - are identified by flashing yellow beacons on both sides of the road and black and white stripes on the crossing. They also have white zigzag markings on both sides of the crossing and a give way line about a yard from the crossing, which marks the place for drivers to stop when necessary.

Pelican crossings - are light-controlled crossings where the pedestrian uses push-button controls to stop the traffic. The crossing area is shown by studs and a stop line marks the place for drivers to stop when necessary.

Puffin crossings - are user-friendly crossings where electronic devices automatically detect when pedestrians are on the crossing. These reduce unnecessary delays in traffic flow.

Toucan crossings - are shared by pedestrians and cyclists. Cyclists are permitted to cycle across.

The flashing yellow beacons at some zebra crossings can be difficult to see in bright sunshine

At a pelican crossing the amber light flashes to give pedestrians enough time to complete crossing before the lights change to green

The rider and crossings

Some rules and advice apply to all types of crossing

- you must not park on the crossing (this blocks the way for pedestrians) or within the area marked by the zigzag lines (this obstructs both the pedestrians' view of approaching vehicles and approaching drivers' view of the crossing)
- you must not overtake the moving motor vehicle nearest the crossing or the leading vehicle which has stopped to give way to a pedestrian
- even if there are no zigzag lines, never overtake just before a crossing
- give yourself more time to stop if the road is wet or icy

- keep the crossing clear when queuing in traffic; stop before the crossing if you can see that you won't be able to clear it
- always allow pedestrians plenty of time to cross, especially if they are elderly or disabled, and do not harass them by revving your engine or edging forward
- watch out for pedestrians who try to rush across at the last minute.

Remember, you should take extra care where the view of either side of the crossing is blocked by queuing traffic. Pedestrians may be crossing between these vehicles, incorrectly thinking they have stopped to allow them to cross

At a puffin crossing there is no flashing amber phase and the lights follow the sequence of traffic lights

Additional rules for different types of crossing

Zebra crossing - Where pedestrians are waiting on the pavement at a zebra crossing and obviously want to cross, slow down and stop to let them cross.

You should stop if you can do so safely, especially

- if anyone is waiting on the pavement with a pram or pushchair
- if children or the elderly are hesitating to cross because of heavy traffic.

You must give way to anyone who is already crossing or has stepped onto the crossing.

Don't wave people across. There could be another vehicle coming in the other direction and you can't be sure what other drivers might do.

Some zebra crossings are divided by a central island. Each half is a separate crossing.

Puffin crossings - Electronic devices automatically detect when pedestrians are on the crossing and delay the green light until the pedestrians have reached a position of safety. If the pedestrians cross quickly, the pedestrian phase is shortened. If the pedestrians have crossed the road before the phase starts, it will automatically be cancelled.

Because the signals are controlled in this way, there is no flashing amber phase.

Toucan crossings - The signals are push-button operated and there is no flashing amber phase.

Pelican crossings - These light-controlled crossings have no red and amber before the green. Instead, they have a flashing amber light which means you must give way to pedestrians on the crossing but, if it's clear, you can go on.

Pelican crossings may be

- straight - a pelican crossing which goes straight across the road is one crossing, even if there is a central refuge. You must wait for people coming from the other side of the refuge
- staggered - if the crossings on each side of the central refuge are not in line, the crossings are separate.

School crossing patrols

Watch out for the patrols and obey their signals.

At particularly dangerous locations, two amber lights flashing alternately give advance warning of the crossing point.

Don't overtake when you're approaching a school crossing and always keep your speed down so you're ready to slow down or stop, if necessary.

Defensive riding - Always look well ahead to identify pedestrian crossings early. Look for the flashing yellow beacons, traffic lights, zigzag markings, etc. Use the OSM/PSL routine and keep your speed well down.

Brake lights cannot be seen by the pedestrians at the crossings or oncoming traffic, so if you're the leading vehicle you should consider using an arm signal when you're slowing or stopping.

You must obey signals given by a school crossing patrol

If it is a sunny day make allowances for lower light levels as you enter a tunnel and be prepared for the dazzle of bright sunshine as you emerge

Tunnels

When approaching a tunnel

- ensure you use your dipped headlights
- stop and remove sunglasses
- observe the road signs and signals
- keep an appropriate distance from the vehicle in front
- if you have a radio fitted, listen to the indicated radio station.

If the tunnel is congested

- switch on your hazard warning lights. Only use them for long enough to ensure your warning has been seen
- keep your distance, even if you are moving slowly or stopped
- if possible, listen out for messages on the radio
- follow any instructions given by tunnel officials or variable message signs.

For action to take in the event of a breakdown or accident see page 238.

Parking

The parking rules in *The Highway Code* also apply to motorcycles. When you park, take care to

- park on firm, level ground. On soft ground the stand can sink, causing the machine to fall over. On a very hot day side or centre stands can sink into tarmac softened by the heat. If your machine falls over it could injure a passer-by or damage another parked vehicle
- use the centre stand if you're leaving your machine for some time
- switch off the fuel tap
- lock the steering and take the ignition key with you.

If you park a sidecar outfit on a gradient make sure that it doesn't roll away. Leave the machine in a low gear and block a wheel or wedge it against the kerb.

Motorcycle parking places

In many towns you can find areas set aside for motorcycle parking. These areas often have fixed metal stands to which you can secure your motorcycle.

Some car parks also set aside areas for motorcycles. Look for signs or marked out parking bays.

Security

While theft of motorcycles is all too common, there are steps you can take to make it difficult for thieves

- if possible park in a car park displaying the Secured Car Park logo. These are car parks that have met the conditions of the police Secured Car Parks scheme. Road signs will indicate their location
- if parking on the road during the day, park in a busy public place
- at night park in a well-lit area
- try not to park in the same place every day
- don't leave your helmet or other possessions with the motorcycle.

When securing your motorcycle always use the steering lock. Additional locking devices include high tension steel cable or chain with a high quality padlock, a U-lock or disc lock.

Fastening your motorcycle to an immovable object or another motorcycle will give extra security.

Other security measures

In addition to locking up your motorcycle you may use other security measures. These include

- fitting an alarm. Make sure the alarm is suitable for your machine. It's a good idea to display a sticker warning that the motorcycle is protected by an alarm - but not the alarm make or model
- having your motorcycle security marked. This involves having the Vehicle Identification Number (VIN) put on the motorcycle. This is unobtrusive and having it put on as many parts as you can will, in the event of theft, help the police to return the motorcycle.

section **nine**
BENDS AND JUNCTIONS

This section covers

- Bends
- Junctions
- The junction routine
- Turning
- Emerging
- Types of junction
- Roundabouts
- Dual carriageways

Bends

Modern roads present a huge variety of bends, corners and junctions – points where the road changes direction.

These are often major hazards, and accident statistics show that no rider can afford to venture out without a thorough knowledge of how to deal with them. The whole of this section is devoted to dealing with bends, corners and junctions safely.

> **Remember,** a bend can feel like a sharp corner to a rider who approaches it too fast - with disastrous results.

Dealing effectively and safely with bends demands that you look well ahead and try to assess accurately how severe the bend is and at what speed you need to be travelling to negotiate it under control.

You should exercise sound judgement and a defensive approach. Where vision is restricted, be prepared to meet

- oncoming vehicles
- obstructions such as broken down or slow moving vehicles
- pedestrians walking on your side of the road.

You should

- control your speed on approach
- choose the right gear for the road speed
- use the throttle carefully
- hold the correct line through the bend.

129

Counter steering

Counter steering is a method of effectively controlling the direction of a machine whilst negotiating hazards such as bends and corners.

It is a technique and skill that should only be taught by professional motorcycle instructors. DSA recommends that the technique should only be introduced at a stage of your training and development that the instructor deems safe and appropriate.

Your speed, position and gear should be correct before you start to turn

Right-hand bends

Keep to the left to improve your view. Watch out for

- drains, gravel and road debris
- uneven or slippery surfaces
- drives and entrances
- road junctions
- adverse camber.

When riding around a right-hand bend, don't ride too close to the centre line. Your head might cross over to the other side of the road as you bank over and you may put yourself into the path of oncoming traffic.

Left-hand bends

On a left-hand bend keep to your normal road position. Moving out to the centre of the road as you approach the bend may give you a slightly improved view, but could endanger you by

- placing you too close to the oncoming traffic
- misleading other road users.

The road camber may work to your advantage, but don't go too fast.

Look out for

- pedestrians, especially when there is no footpath
- horse riders
- stationary or broken down vehicles
- oncoming vehicles crossing the centre line
- vehicles waiting to turn right.

Always ride at such a speed that you can stop safely in the distance you can see to be clear.

Speed

Judging the correct road speed as you approach bends and corners takes practice and experience.

That speed will depend on the

- type and condition of the road
- sharpness of the bend
- camber of the road
- visibility
- weather conditions.

Camber - The camber of a road is the angle at which the road normally slopes away from the centre to help drainage.

On a left-hand bend the camber helps by reducing the angle between the tyre and the road.

On a right-hand bend the opposite is true and the increased angle between tyre and road can lead to reduced stability.

Adverse camber - Here the road slopes downwards towards the outside of the corner. The forces acting on your motorcycle could cause reduced stability due to

- the increased angle between tyre and road surface
- the road sloping away from the direction of turn.

Banking - On a few bends, such as some motorway slip roads, the road slopes upwards towards the outside of the bend. This applies across the whole width of the road but here traffic is usually restricted to travelling in one direction only.

The correct speed is the one which takes your motorcycle around the bend under full control with the greatest safety for you, your passenger and other road users

Adjusting your speed

Don't go into a bend too fast. Reduce speed before you enter the bend.

You can reduce your speed by rolling off the throttle, and

- allowing the road speed to fall
- using the brakes progressively and, if necessary, changing to a lower gear.

Your speed should be at its lowest as you begin to turn.

Braking on a bend - Avoid braking on a bend.

If you must brake on a bend

- avoid using the front brake. Rely on the rear brake and engine braking to slow you down. If you must use the front brake, be very gentle. There's a risk of the front tyre losing its grip and sliding sideways
- try to bring your motorcycle upright and brake normally (provided you can do so safely).

Your speed should take into account unseen hazards, such as changes in the road surface or the possibility of pedestrians

Using the throttle

Don't confuse 'using the throttle' with 'accelerating', which means going faster. When dealing with bends 'using the throttle' means using it just enough to make the engine drive the motorcycle around the bend.

The correct speed at a corner or bend will depend on a number of things, including

- how sharp it is
- your view
- road conditions
- other traffic.

Taking everything into account, you will have to judge

- the correct position
- the proper speed for the corner or bend
- the gear most suitable for that speed.

The secret of dealing with bends is to make sure that

- your speed is at its lowest before you start the turn
- you use the throttle so that the engine is doing just enough work to drive the motorcycle around the bend without going faster.

Caution - Too much throttle can cause the rear tyre to lose grip and skid.

As you leave the bend and can see further ahead you can increase your speed to suit the road and traffic conditions.

Gears

Make sure you select the correct gear before you enter the bend. The correct gear will depend on a number of factors including

- your speed
- road conditions
- other traffic
- warning signs and road markings.

Load

Any change in the centre of gravity or weight the motorcycle is carrying will affect its handling on bends, compared with when it's lightly loaded.

This change may be caused by

- a pillion passenger
- carrying heavy objects
- incorrect tyre pressure.

Negotiating bends

Look ahead - Look well ahead for any indications, such as road signs, warnings and road markings, which will tell you

- the type of bend
- the direction the road takes
- how sharp the bend is
- whether the bend is one of a series.

Assess the situation - Ask yourself

- how dangerous does it seem? Remember, the word 'Slow' is painted on the road for good reason.
- are there likely to be obstructions on the bend? For example, slow moving vehicles or parked cars.
- are there likely to be pedestrians on your side of the road? Is there a footpath?
- what's the camber like? Look well ahead - it's too late to find out in the middle of the bend when your brakes can't help you.

Always ride so you can stop safely within the limit of your vision. Take extra care where your view is restricted.

Approach with care

- As you approach, follow the OSM/PSL routine
- Before you reach the bend take up the best approach position for the type of bend and adjust your speed, if necessary, and select the most suitable gear.

Entering the bend - As you enter the bend, use the throttle just enough to keep

- the tyres gripping
- full control.

After you begin to turn - Avoid braking, except in an emergency.

Stopping on a bend

Avoid stopping on a bend, except in an emergency. If you have to stop, either

- get your motorcycle off the road, or
- stop where following traffic can see you. This is especially important on left-hand bends, where vision can be more limited.

If you can, stop clear of a continuous centre line.

A series of bends

Double and multiple bends are almost always signed. Take note of road signs and road markings.

For example, if the second bend followed closely after the first and you haven't taken notice of the road signs or markings, you could find yourself speeding up when you should be slowing down. This can result in hasty replanning and loss of control.

On a winding road, use your gears sensibly and select the appropriate gear for the speed. This will enable you to ride at a safe speed while keeping the right amount of load on the engine and maximum grip on the road.

Bends in series often swing in alternate directions. As soon as you have negotiated one, you have to prepare for the next. Look well ahead for changes in the camber of the road, which could affect your control.

At night

On unfamiliar roads, the lights of oncoming traffic may help you to plan ahead. However, negotiating bends at night has its own hazards. Ride with extra care, and

- be prepared for hazards around the bend
- be prepared to be affected by the lights of oncoming traffic, especially on right-hand bends. Don't be taken by surprise
- dip your headlights in advance for oncoming traffic approaching the bend, especially on left-hand bends.

Defensive riding

Always be on the lookout for other vehicles creating dangerous situations. Stay well clear of trouble, such as

- a vehicle overtaking too close to a bend
- a vehicle approaching a bend too fast
- oncoming vehicles straddling the centre lines
- oncoming vehicles skidding in bad weather
- a vehicle waiting to turn into a concealed entrance.

Junctions

A junction is where two or more roads meet. Junctions are hazards where there is a greater risk of an accident occurring. Treat them with great care, no matter how easy they look. There are five main types of junction

- T-junctions
- Y-junctions
- staggered junctions
- crossroads
- roundabouts.

Advance information

Look for information about the junction ahead, and the level of difficulty, such as

- the amount of traffic
- warning signs
- road markings

- direction signs
- Give Way and Stop signs
- traffic lights
- a break in the line of buildings
- changes in road surface.

Approaching junctions

How you approach a junction depends on what you intend to do. You might want to

- cross a major road going ahead
- emerge into a major road by turning right
- emerge into a major road by turning left
- leave a major road by turning right or left into a minor road
- stay on a major road and pass the junction.

A major road is one with priority over another at a junction.

Priority

Usually, road signs and markings indicate priority. Where no priority is shown at a junction, take extra care.

Lanes at junction

When you approach a junction

- do so in the correct lane for the direction you intend to take; don't switch lanes to gain advantage
- look well ahead and watch for traffic and direction signs
- look out for signals from vehicles about to change lanes
- look out for vehicles suddenly changing lanes without signalling.

Articulated or long vehicles

Stay clear of large vehicles at junctions. These need much more room than smaller vehicles, and may take up a position that seems incorrect to you.

They often swing out to the right before turning left, and to the left before turning right. At junctions and roundabouts don't be tempted to squeeze past. The rear wheels might cut across your path as the vehicle turns.

Be ready for them to stop if their way is blocked.

Passing minor roads

Look out for road signs indicating minor roads, even if you're not turning off.

Watch out for emerging vehicles. Their view is often obscured at junctions. A vehicle might pull out in front of you.

If this happens, and you're not sure the driver has seen you, slow down. Be prepared to stop.

Be tolerant and don't harass the other driver by sounding your horn aggressively or riding too close.

Overtaking

Don't overtake at, or approaching, a junction.

The road surface at junctions

Always watch out for slippery surfaces or loose chippings. Avoid braking while you're turning. Plan ahead - brake before the junction.

Defensive riding - Adjust your overall speed when passing a series of minor roads so you can stop within the distance you can see to be clear.

The junction routine should enable you to cope with all likelihoods at road junctions

The junction routine

At every junction use the OSM/PSL routine.

Observation - Look all around so that you're aware of the traffic situation.

Signal - You should signal clearly and in good time.

Manoeuvre - Use the PSL routine:

Position - If the road has no lane markings

- when turning left, keep to the left
- when turning right, keep as close to the centre of the road as is safe. In a one-way street move to the right-hand side of the road in good time.

If the road has lane markings

- use the correct lane for the direction you intend to take
- move into the lane as soon as you can.

Speed - Adjust your speed as necessary.

Look - Watch for other traffic when you reach a point from which you can see.

In traffic, don't lose your patience or switch lanes to gain advantage over others.

When you're moving ahead

- make sure that you're in the correct lane
- look out for vehicles changing lane, either with or without signalling.

Turning

Turning right into a side road

Assess the junction and use the OSM/PSL routine. Check the road signs and markings.

Observation - Look in your mirrors and take rear observation as necessary.

Signal - Signal right in good time.

Manoeuvre - Use the PSL routine:

Position - Position yourself as close to the centre of the road as is safe, so that vehicles can pass on your left. In a one-way street, keep to the right-hand side of the road.

Speed - Adjust your speed as necessary. Watch out for approaching traffic. Stop if necessary.

Look - Look into the road you're joining. Watch for vehicles waiting to emerge and pedestrians crossing the road.

Take a 'lifesaver' glance over your right shoulder just before you turn. Do this early enough for you to change your plan if it isn't safe to turn.

Avoid cutting the corner (enter on the left-hand side of the road).

When you've completed the turn

- cancel your signal
- check for traffic behind you
- accelerate progressively up to the speed suitable for the road and traffic conditions within the set speed limit.

Turning left into a side road - Assess the junction and use the OSM/PSL routine. Check the road signs and markings.

Observation - Look in your mirrors and take rear observation as necessary.

Signal - Signal left at the correct time.

Manoeuvre - Use the PSL routine:

Position - Your position on approach may not change significantly from your normal riding position but could be affected by factors such as

- parked vehicles or other obstructions
- other road users
- road markings
- the road surface
- the road width.

Speed - Left turns are often sharper than right turns, so reduce speed accordingly.

Look - Look out for vehicles stopping just before the junction and pedestrians who may not have seen you. Don't overtake a cyclist just before the turn and then cut in just ahead. If you're riding slowly, watch for cyclists coming up on your left - a lifesaver glance over your left shoulder before you turn may be necessary. Take special care when

- crossing a bicycle or bus lane
- pedestrians are crossing or waiting to cross, especially children
- on a loose or slippery road surface.

When you've completed the turn

- cancel your signal
- check behind so that you know what's following
- adopt the correct road position
- accelerate progressively up to the speed suitable for the road and traffic conditions within the set speed limit.

Emerging

Emerging is when a vehicle leaves one road and joins, crosses or turns into another.

You'll have to judge the speed and distance of any traffic on the road you intend to emerge into, and only continue when it's safe to do so.

This needs care and sometimes patience as well.

When to go

You have to decide when to wait and when it's safe to go. That decision depends largely on your zone of vision.

Your zone of vision is what you can see from your position. It is determined by

- buildings and hedges
- bends in the road or contours in the land
- moving and parked vehicles
- available light and the weather.

As you approach a junction, your zone of vision onto the other road usually improves. The last few feet can be critical.

You can only decide whether to wait or go on when you have put yourself in a position where you can see clearly.

If another vehicle or a pedestrian is not in your zone of vision, you're not usually in theirs.

Sometimes parked vehicles interfere with your zone of vision so that you have to inch carefully forward to see more

Looking means that you need to assess the situation, decide whether it's safe and act accordingly.

After you emerge

- make sure that you cancel your signal
- check behind for the speed and position of other traffic
- accelerate so that your speed is correct for the road and conditions
- keep a safe distance from the vehicle in front.

Give Way signs or lines

A Give Way sign and lines across the road means that you must give way to traffic which is already on the road you intend to enter.

If you can emerge without causing drivers or riders on that road to alter speed or course, you can do so without stopping. Otherwise, you must stop.

Stop signs

You must always stop at a Stop sign no matter what the traffic situation seems on the road you intend to enter. Move off only when you have a clear view and you're sure it's safe.

Junctions without signs or road markings

Treat these with great care.

Don't assume you have priority at an unmarked junction.

Other traffic

Bends and hills could make it more difficult to see traffic coming towards you.

If the vehicle approaching from your right is signalling to turn left into your road, wait until you're sure the vehicle is turning and not pulling up on the left beyond your road or that the driver has forgotten to cancel their last signal.

Stop signs are often placed at junctions where the visibility is limited. Once you have stopped you may still need to edge forward for a clear view

Emerging left into a major road

Assess the junction. Check the road signs and markings. Use the OSM/PSL routine

Observation - Look in your mirrors and take rear observation as necessary.

Signal - Signal left at the correct time.

Manoeuvre - Use the PSL routine:

Position - Position - keep to the left.

Speed - Reduce speed - Be prepared to stop. Traffic on a minor road must give way to traffic on a major road.

Look - Look in all directions at the earliest point from which you can see. Keep looking as you slow down, and stop if necessary.

> **Remember,** an approaching vehicle, particularly a bus or a lorry, can easily mask another moving vehicle that may be overtaking.

You must be aware of pedestrians, cyclists and other motorcyclists who may be alongside. You also need to know how traffic behind is reacting to your manoeuvre.

Emerging right into a major road

Assess the junction. Check road signs and markings. Use the OSM/PSL routine

Observation - Look in your mirrors and take rear observation as necessary.

Signal - Signal right in good time.

Manoeuvre - Use the PSL routine:

Position - Position yourself as close to the centre of the road as is safe

- in a one-way street, position yourself on the right-hand side of the road
- when turning right it's important to take up your position early.

Speed - Reduce speed. Be prepared to stop. You must give way to traffic on a major road.

Look - Look in all directions at the earliest point from which you can see. Keep looking as you slow down, and stop if necessary.

Watch out for

- traffic turning across your path
- pedestrians.

Types of junction

Each type of junction can have many variations.

What you intend to do at the junction determines how you approach each type.

T-junctions

You'll find these where a minor road joins a major road from the left or right. The minor road will have either

- a Stop sign and road markings
- a Give Way sign and road markings
- Give Way lines only
- no road signs or markings.

If you're riding on the major road

- take note of any road signs and markings
- watch for vehicles turning or emerging
- avoid overtaking on the approach to a T-junction.

If you're riding on the minor road

- take note of the road signs
- look for slippery surfaces or loose chippings
- stop before emerging if your view into the major road is blocked in any way.

Hatch markings - On busier roads, the major road is often split before and after the junction, with a turn-right filter lane protected by white diagonal hatch markings (or chevrons) surrounded by a broken or an unbroken white line.

Join and leave the major road at these junctions exactly as you would a dual carriageway.

Warning - Areas of hatch markings are painted on the road

- to separate streams of traffic
- to protect traffic waiting to turn right.

Remember, painted road markings can be slippery especially when wet.

Where the boundary line is solid, do not enter except in an emergency.

Where the boundary line is broken, you should not ride on these markings unless you can see it's safe to do so.

Junctions on bends - Look well ahead for traffic signs and road markings which indicate priority. These junctions need extra care, especially when turning right from a major road which bends to the left, because

- your field of vision might be limited
- traffic might be approaching at speed from your left
- you'll need time to manoeuvre safely.

Your position before you turn must not endanger either oncoming traffic or yourself.

Wait until there's a gap in the traffic and act positively.

Unmarked junctions - Never assume priority over another road if there are no road signs or markings. What's obvious to you might not be obvious to drivers on the other road.

Watch carefully for vehicles

- approaching the junction on the other road
- waiting at the junction
- emerging from the junction to join or cross your path.

Remember, any vehicle crossing

- might assume priority and expect you to give way
- might not assume priority, but might have misjudged your speed or not seen you.

Such a vehicle creates a hazard.

You should respond in a safe and sensible manner. Anticipate and adjust your speed accordingly to avoid an accident.

Y-junctions

At a Y-junction the minor road joins the major road at an acute angle. Y-junctions can be deceptive because they often call for little change in direction.

Normally the road going straight ahead has priority and joining roads have either Give Way or Stop signs. However, there are many exceptions.

Watch out for oncoming vehicles positioned incorrectly. The drivers might have misjudged the junction.

Going straight ahead on the major road -

- Look well ahead for road signs and markings.
- Watch out for vehicles emerging to turn left or right.
- Never overtake when approaching any junction.

Emerging onto the major road - If the angle of approach to the major road is very sharp and from the right, the view to your left might be restricted.

If you position your motorcycle towards the major road at a right angle as you approach the Stop or Give Way lines, you will improve your view.

Staggered junctions

These are junctions where roads join from both right and left. At a staggered junction the side roads don't join directly opposite one another but are slightly offset.

If you're riding on the major road look for

- advance warning signs
- vehicles emerging from either side
- traffic turning into the side roads
- vehicles crossing from one minor road into another.

If you're emerging from either minor road

- watch for traffic approaching in both directions
- watch for traffic emerging from the road opposite
- look for slippery surfaces.

If you're crossing from one minor road into another take extra care. If there's room and it's safe, emerge to the centre of the major road and wait for a safe opportunity to complete the manoeuvre.

If there isn't enough room, make sure that the gap in the traffic is wide enough in both directions for you to cross the major road safely. If in doubt, wait.

At crossroads look for other road users who may not give way

Crossroads

Crossroads are often accident blackspots, so take extra care, especially on roads carrying fast moving traffic.

Accidents often involve vehicles turning right. The procedure when turning at crossroads is much the same as at any other junction.

You'll need to assess the crossroads on approach, so look well ahead and check for road signs and markings which might indicate priority.

Riding on the major road - Watch for road signs and markings. Also watch for emerging traffic. Be especially careful of vehicles trying to cut across, using gaps in the traffic. They may misjudge your speed or not see you at all. Adjust your speed approaching crossroads.

Turning right - Getting your position and speed correct is vital. Look out for traffic on the road you're joining as well as on the road you're leaving.

> **Remember,** a 'lifesaver' glance before starting to turn, especially if you've had to wait.

Turning right when an oncoming vehicle is also turning right - When two vehicles approaching from opposite directions both want to turn right there are two methods that can be used. Either method is acceptable, but will usually be determined by

- the layout of the crossroads
- what course the other driver decides to take
- road markings.

147

At some crossroads road markings direct turning nearside to nearside

Turning offside to offside - The advantage of this method is that both can see oncoming traffic. In congested conditions, leave a space for approaching traffic to turn right.

Turning nearside to nearside - This method is less safe because the view of oncoming vehicles is not clear. Watch out for oncoming traffic hidden by larger vehicles and be ready to stop. Police control or road markings sometimes make this method compulsory.

Defensive riding - Try and make eye contact with the driver of the approaching vehicle to determine which course is best. Your speed should allow you to stop if the other driver cuts across your path.

Approaching on a minor road - If you approach the crossroads on one of the minor roads and want to turn onto the major road, as long as the minor road

opposite is clear, you should treat it as if you are emerging from a T-junction.

If you want to turn onto the major road, and another vehicle is approaching the crossroads from the minor road opposite, then if you are turning

- left or going straight on, you should proceed with extra caution and make sure no vehicle from the opposite direction is going to cross your path

- right and the other vehicle is going ahead or turning left, you should normally wait for the other vehicle to clear the junction before you make your turn, because you would otherwise be cutting across their path

- right and the other vehicle is turning right, you should try to make eye contact with the other driver to establish who should proceed as neither of you has priority.

Unmarked crossroads

Treat unmarked crossroads with extreme caution since neither road affords priority.

Priority - Never assume you have priority if there are no signs or markings.

Drivers approaching on other roads might also assume they have priority, and an accident could result.

Proceed only when you're sure it's safe to do so.

Remember, you must look, assess and decide, before you act.

Take extra care when your view is restricted (by vehicles, walls, hedges, etc.).

Passing side roads

Look out for road signs indicating side roads, even if you aren't turning off. Often views are obscured at urban junctions. A driver may not see you and pull out in front of you.

If you doubt that a driver in a side road has seen you, slow down and sound your horn. Be prepared to stop, if necessary.

Make yourself easy to see. Wear bright clothing and have your headlamp on dipped beam at all times.

Even if a waiting driver appears to have seen you, ride defensively and be prepared to stop if necessary

Roundabouts

Roundabouts allow traffic from different roads to merge or cross without necessarily stopping.

Priority

Before you enter a roundabout, you normally give way to any traffic approaching from your immediate right. However, you should keep moving if the way is clear.

In a few cases, traffic on the roundabout has to give way to traffic entering. Look out for Give Way signs and road markings on the roundabout.

Some roundabouts have traffic lights (sometimes part-time) which determine priority.

Always use the OSM/PSL routine on approach.

Approaching a roundabout

Always look well ahead for the advance warning sign, especially at large or complex roundabouts. This will give you a clear picture of the layout of the roundabout, together with route directions.

The sign will enable you to select the most suitable lane in which to approach the roundabout.

Watch out also for advance warnings of appropriate traffic lanes at the roundabout. These are often backed up by road markings, which usually include route numbers, so

* get into the correct lane in good time
* don't straddle lanes
* never change lanes at the last moment.

Where possible it's a good idea to look across the roundabout and identify the exit you're aiming to take. This will help you to plan the safest course on the roundabout itself.

Procedure

Adopt the following procedure unless road signs or markings indicate otherwise.

Going left - You should

* take effective rear observation
* indicate left as you approach
* approach in the left-hand lane
* keep to that lane on the roundabout
* maintain a left-turn signal through the roundabout.

Using the OSM/PSL routine should ensure that you arrive at a roundabout ready to give way to traffic approaching from the right or to keep moving if the way is clear

Going ahead - You should

- take effective rear observation
- not signal on approach
- approach in the left-hand lane. If you can't use the left-hand lane because, for example, it's blocked, use the next lane to it
- keep to the selected lane on the roundabout
- take effective rear observation to the nearside or offside as appropriate
- indicate left just after you have passed the exit before the one you intend to take
- if you have to cross a lane on your left to reach your exit take a 'lifesaver' glance to the nearside before changing direction.

Going right or full circle - You should

- take effective rear observation
- indicate right as you approach
- approach in the right-hand lane
- keep to that lane and maintain the signal on the roundabout

> **Remember,** when using the right-hand lane to go ahead or when turning right, be aware of traffic in the lane to your left.

- take rear observation especially to the nearside
- indicate left just after you have passed the exit before the one you intend to take
- if you have to cross a lane on your left to reach your exit, take a 'lifesaver' glance to the nearside before changing direction.

More than three lanes - Where there are more than three lanes at the approach to the roundabout, use the most appropriate lane on approach and through the roundabout, unless road signs or markings tell you otherwise.

Defensive riding

Always keep an eye on the vehicle in front as you're about to enter the roundabout, they may stop while you're still looking to the right. Many rear-end collisions happen this way. Make sure the vehicle has actually moved away.

Hazards

Roundabouts can be particularly hazardous areas. While negotiating the roundabout you should be especially aware of

- pedestrians - in many areas, zebra crossings are located near the entrances and exits to roundabouts. Even if there are no formal crossings, pedestrians may attempt to cross the road at these junctions. Always be aware of pedestrians who may be trying to cross the road

- cyclists and horseriders - they often keep to the outside of the roundabout even when intending to turn right. Take extra care and allow them plenty of room

Make sure you get into the correct lane for the exit you wish to take in good time

- long vehicles - because of their length, they might take a different course as they approach the roundabout and as they go round it. Watch out for their signals and allow for the rear of their vehicle cutting in

- all vehicles - be prepared for vehicles to cross your path to leave at the next exit. Always be on the lookout for their signals

- road surfaces - these can become very slippery, particularly when wet. Also as vehicles travel around roundabouts and bends fuel can spill onto the road. In wet weather diesel and oil spillage can be seen as a rainbow coloured pattern across the road. Even in dry conditions, diesel and oil spillage makes the surface slippery. If you smell diesel, be particularly careful.

Mini roundabouts

Approach these in the same way as a roundabout, but remember, there's less space to manoeuvre and less time to signal. For example, there's often insufficient time to signal left when leaving.

You must pass round the central markings and you should also

- give way to oncoming vehicles turning right
- be sure any vehicle on the roundabout is going to leave it before you join it
- beware of drivers who are using the roundabout for a U-turn.

Double mini roundabouts - Treat each roundabout separately and give way to traffic from your right. Also, take careful all-round observation before you enter.

Multiple roundabouts

At some complex junctions, a large roundabout can incorporate a series of mini roundabouts at the intersections.

You need to take extra care because traffic can be travelling in all directions around the large roundabout.

Look and assess - Keep a good look out and assess the situation at each mini roundabout. Look for direction signs and lane markings well in advance.

Dual carriageways

These are roads which have a central reservation dividing streams of traffic. There may also be a safety barrier on the central reservation.

Although some dual carriageways appear similar to motorways, the same regulations don't apply.

> **Remember,** traffic may be travelling faster than on a single carriageway.

Beware of slow-moving vehicles such as farm tractors, cyclists and pedestrians.

Turning left from a dual carriageway

If there's no deceleration lane or slip road

- signal your intentions clearly and in good time
- slow down in good time.

If there's a deceleration lane or slip road

- signal in good time
- don't reduce speed until you've moved into the deceleration lane
- check your speedometer. If you've been riding at high speeds you may find yourself travelling faster than you realise.

Turning left onto a dual carriageway

If there's no acceleration lane or slip road

- emerge as you would to turn left on a single carriageway

If there's an acceleration lane or slip road

- emerge as you would to join a motorway (see page 173)
- use the acceleration lane to increase speed. Match your speed with that of traffic in the left-hand lane

- move into a safe gap in the traffic
- remember to use a lifesaver glance just before you move into the left lane.

Only wait in the central reservation if it's wide enough for you to wait safely.

Turning right onto a dual carriageway

You'll have to cross the first carriageway before you can join the carriageway you want.

If the central reservation is wide enough

- you can wait in it for a gap in the traffic on the carriageway you want
- don't leave yourself jutting out either side of the central reservation.

If the central reservation is too narrow, wait until the dual carriageway is clear in both directions.

Turning right from a dual carriageway

The central reservation sometimes has gaps for turning right. These may have special filter lanes.

> **Remember,** traffic may be travelling at high speeds. If in doubt, wait for a large gap in the traffic.

To turn right, use your mirrors and signal in good time. Don't forget a lifesaver glance before you turn.

You may have to cross the path of fast oncoming vehicles in two or more lanes. If in doubt, wait.

155

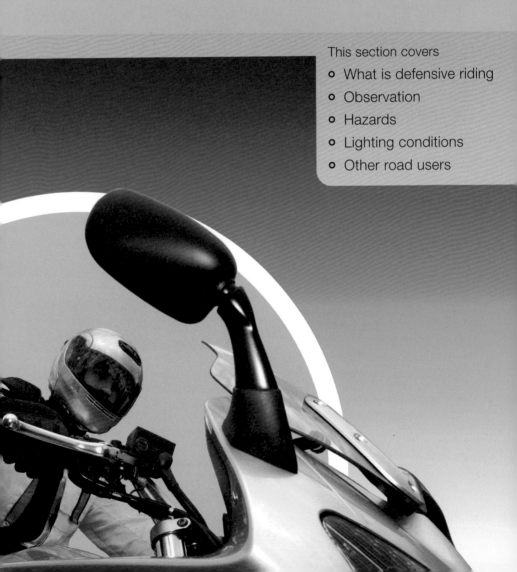

section **ten**
DEFENSIVE RIDING

This section covers

o What is defensive riding

o Observation

o Hazards

o Lighting conditions

o Other road users

What is defensive riding

On today's roads it's important that you look and plan well ahead. Avoid putting yourself in a situation where you're trying to do too many things at once.

Anticipation is a skill which develops with experience. This section describes the main features of defensive riding which will help you to gain that experience safely. Use these techniques whenever you ride.

Defensive riding is based on effective observation, good anticipation and control. It's about always questioning the actions of other road users and being prepared for the unexpected, so as not to be taken by surprise. Defensive riding involves

* awareness
* planning
* anticipating
* staying in control.

This means understanding the responsibility that comes with riding and showing consideration and courtesy.

Safety above all else - It's about having real concern, not only for your own safety, but also for other road users, including the most vulnerable. Expect other people to make mistakes, and be ready to slow down or stop – even if you think you have priority. Never rely on other road users doing the correct thing.

Your safety - Your safety lies mainly in your own hands. The better your control of your motorcycle and road space, the safer you'll be. Your riding should always set a good example to other road users.

You never know when your good example will make a deep impression on another rider, especially a learner or inexperienced rider, and perhaps save lives in the future.

Reducing hostility

With defensive riding, you show patience and anticipation. This helps to reduce the number of incidents which result in

* open hostility
* abusive language
* threats
* physical violence.

Avoid the kind of riding that

* gives offence to other road users
* provokes reaction
* creates dangerous situations.

Competitive riding

Never ride in a spirit of competition. Competitive riding is, inherently, the opposite of defensive riding. It increases the risks to everyone.

Observation

When you take rear observation, just looking is not enough. You must act sensibly on what you see.

You must make a mental note of the speed, behaviour and possible intentions of any other road user. If you're not observing effectively, you can't assess a traffic situation correctly.

At junctions, there's no point in just looking if your view is obstructed - for example, by parked vehicles. You must also move carefully into a position where you can see without emerging into the path of oncoming traffic.

Look, assess and decide before you act.

That's what effective observation is all about.

Observing what's ahead

A skillful rider constantly watches and interprets what's happening ahead.

Always ride at such a speed that you can stop safely within the distance you can see to be clear. A good rider will constantly scan the road ahead and to the side and, by use of effective rear observation, be aware of the situation behind.

Approaching a bend - Ask yourself

- can I see the full picture?
- how sharply does it bend?
- am I in the right position?
- is my speed right?
- what might I meet?
- could I stop if I had to?

Approaching a junction - Ask yourself

- have I seen the whole junction?
- can others see me?
- am I sure they've seen me?
- have I got an escape route if they haven't?

Don't ride beyond the limits of your vision.

Zone of vision at a junction

Your zone of vision is what you can see as you look forward and to the side from your position. As you approach a junction, your zone of vision onto the other road usually improves.

You may need to get very close before you can look far enough into another road to see if it's safe to proceed. The last few feet are often critical.

Sometimes parked vehicles restrict your view so much that you need to stop and inch forward for a proper view before you emerge.

- Look in every direction before you emerge.
- Keep looking as you join the other road.
- Be ready to stop.
- Use all the information available to you - look through the windows of parked vehicles.
- Use the reflections in shop windows to observe oncoming traffic.

Screen pillar obstruction - The windscreen pillars can cause obstructions to a driver's view of the road. You should be aware of this effect, particularly when emerging from junctions.

Other road users - It can be difficult to see some other road users, especially when you are emerging from a junction. Those who are particularly at risk are

- pedestrians - they frequently cross at a junction and often find it difficult to judge the speed and course of approaching traffic

Remember, never rely solely on a quick glance - give yourself time to take in the whole scene.

- cyclists - they can be difficult to see, because they can easily be obscured by trees and other objects, especially if they are riding close to the side of the road. They might be approaching at a higher speed than you expect
- other motorcyclists - like cyclists, they are often less easy to see than other motor vehicles.

If another vehicle or a pedestrian is not in your zone of vision, you're not usually in theirs.

Making eye contact with other road users helps you to judge whether they have seen you.

Being seen

As you approach a junction where you can see a vehicle waiting to emerge, ask yourself

- Has the driver seen me?
- What if I haven't been seen?

Many accidents happen at road junctions when a driver doesn't see a motorcyclist.

Daytime use of dipped headlamps and wearing bright clothing increase your chances of being seen.

Observing traffic behind you

You should always know as much as you can about the traffic behind you.

Before you move off, change direction or change speed, you must know how your action will affect other road users. You must also be aware of traffic likely to overtake.

Timing your rear observation - Look behind before you signal your intention or make any manoeuvre. For example, before

- moving off
- changing direction
- turning right or left
- overtaking
- changing lanes
- slowing or stopping (see page 104).

Just looking is not enough - You must act sensibly on what you see, and take note of the speed, behaviour and possible intentions of traffic behind you.

Other road user's blind spot - Avoid riding in another road user's blind spot for any longer than necessary.

Approaching traffic lights

If they are already green ask yourself

- how long have they been on green?
- are there many vehicles already waiting at either side of the junction? If there's a queue, the lights are probably about to change
- do I have time to stop?
- can the vehicle behind me stop? If it's a large goods vehicle, it might need a greater distance to pull up.

Remember, another driver might anticipate the signals by accelerating while the lights are still showing red and amber.

Don't try to beat the traffic signals by accelerating or leave it until the last moment to brake – harsh braking causes skids.

Faulty traffic lights - Where traffic signals are not working, treat the situation as you would an unmarked junction and proceed with great care.

Hazards

*Effective observation and anticipation enable
you to see the clues and respond safely*

A hazard is any situation which could
involve adjusting speed or changing course.
To identify a hazard, you must look well
ahead for clues such as

• road signs

• changes in road conditions

• parked vehicles

• junctions

• other road users.

As soon as you've recognised a hazard,
you must use the mirrors or look behind to
assess how drivers behind you will affect
your planning and how your actions will
affect those drivers.

Allowing time and space

Always leave yourself enough time and
space to cope with what's ahead.

• Keep your eyes scanning the far and
near distance, especially in towns, where
things change quickly.

• Check regularly on traffic behind you.

• Watch for clues about what's going to
happen next.

For example, a parked car could spell
danger if the driver is sitting in it, or you see
vapour from the exhaust in cold weather.
This could indicate that

• a door might open suddenly

• the car might pull out without warning.

If you can see underneath a parked vehicle,
and you can see feet at the other side, a
pedestrian might appear suddenly.

Separation distances

Always keep a good separation distance between you and the vehicle in front.

Leave a gap of at least one metre or yard for each mph of your speed, or use the two-second rule (see page 114).

In bad conditions, leave at least double the distance or a four-second time gap.

Tailgating - When a vehicle behind is too close to you, ease off very gradually and increase the gap between you and the vehicle in front.

Large vehicles - Take extra care when following large vehicles, especially at roundabouts, junctions, entrances, etc.

The driver might have to take a course that seems incorrect to you. For example, moving out to the right before turning left.

Keep well back from any large vehicles that are in the process of manoeuvring to the left or right.

> **Remember,** if you are following too close behind a large vehicle, the driver might not be able to see you in their mirrors.

Don't get caught out by trying to pass on the left.

Large vehicles can also block your view. Your ability to see and plan ahead will be improved if you keep back.

You need to take account of the changing priority of hazards

Recognising hazards

Recognising, prioritising and responding correctly to hazards are skills that develop with experience. It's important to allow enough time and space to see and respond to a hazard before it develops into real danger.

To say you have to see the hazard may sound obvious but it requires you to be looking in the right place. This is why you should be scanning the road ahead constantly varying your attention from near to far distance while also making frequent mirror checks to keep you up to date with the situation behind.

Once you have identified a hazard you will need to take some form of action and this will vary from one hazard to another. Any action which involves a change of speed or course is called a manoeuvre.

A manoeuvre can vary from slowing slightly to turning on a very busy road.

The defensive rider is always

- in the correct position
- travelling at the correct speed for the road, traffic and weather conditions
- in the right gear
- anticipating and prepared for the next change in the traffic situation.

Country roads

These roads present their own hazards. Take extra care and reduce your speed as you approach bends and junctions.

Bends and junctions - Bends can often be sharper than you think they are going to be. They may also obscure other, more vulnerable road users, such as pedestrians, horse riders and cyclists, or larger slow-moving farm vehicles.

Junctions, especially minor junctions or entrances to farm premises, are not always signed and may be partially hidden.

Road surfaces - On country roads be prepared to find

- worn road surfaces
- mud
- hedge cuttings
- leaves in the autumn.

If you see mud or hedge cuttings on the road, anticipate finding the cause around the next bend. This may be farm machinery or farm animals. Either way it will be a slow moving hazard and you need to be prepared to stop.

Other road users - In rural areas there are often no pavements or footpaths on the side of the road and pedestrians are advised to walk on the right-hand side of the road so that they can see oncoming traffic. You should therefore be prepared to find people walking or jogging on your side of the road.

Horse riders and cyclists are often found on country roads. Give them plenty of space and always be patient and wait until it is safe before overtaking, especially on narrow or winding roads.

Approaching any hazard

Follow the OSM/PSL routine every time you recognise a hazard

Observation - Check the position of following traffic using your mirrors or by looking behind at an appropriate time.

Signal - If necessary, signal your intention to change course or slow down. Signal clearly and in good time.

Manoeuvre - Carry out the manoeuvre if it's still safe to do so. Manoeuvre has three phases: Position, Speed and Look.

Position - Get into the correct position in good time to negotiate the hazard. This helps other road users to anticipate what you intend to do.

Positioning yourself too late can be dangerous.

Ask yourself

- can I see and be seen?
- are other vehicles restricting my course of action?
- have I enough room to get out of any difficulties?

Avoid cutting in front of other drivers or riders. If lanes are closed or narrow because of road works, move into the correct lane in good time.

Speed - Ask yourself

- could I stop in time if the vehicle in front suddenly brakes sharply?
- am I going too fast for the road conditions?
- am I in the right gear needed to keep control?

Be prepared to slow down as you approach a hazard and always be ready to stop.

Look - Keep looking ahead to assess all possible dangers.

This is particularly important at a junction.

Look in all directions, even if you're not turning.

If you're joining a road, keep looking as you turn from one road to the other.

Watch out for

- traffic turning across your path
- pedestrians.

Lighting conditions

In the dark, seeing hazards is more difficult. The clues are there, but you have to pick them out. Look for

- illuminated or reflective road signs
- reflectors between white lines
- the glow of vehicle headlights on buildings, trees and hedges indicating bends and junctions.

In the dark

- it can be difficult to judge distances and speed from headlights
- headlights on vehicles make it difficult to see pedestrians, cyclists and any vehicle with dim lights
- don't let shop and advertising lights distract you
- watch for zebra crossings, traffic lights and road signs.

Wet roads

Wet roads increase reflected and distracting light. The reflections from wet surfaces make it more difficult to see unlit objects.

The combination of rain and darkness reduces visibility further. On unlit or poorly lit roads keep your speed down. Remember, your stopping distance will be increased while your visibility is reduced.

Unlit side view

When you're sideways on to other road users you'll be less easily seen, for example when passing side turnings or emerging right or left.

Wearing reflective material will help other drivers to see you.

Other road users

Cyclists

Make allowances for cyclists. They have every right to be on the road. Allow them plenty of room.

The younger the cyclist, the more you must watch them.

Cyclists might

- glance round, showing they might be about to move out or turn
- make sudden sideways movements into your path
- be carrying objects which may affect their control and balance
- struggle on hills, weaving, slowing down or stopping
- swerve round potholes or inspection covers
- have problems in bad weather, particularly strong crosswinds
- have difficulties on poor road surfaces or where tramlines are set in the road.

Powered vehicles used by disabled people

These small vehicles can be used on the pavement and on the road. They are extremely vulnerable when they are on the road because of

- their small size, especially their low height
- their low speed (they have a maximum speed of 8 mph).

They are often not easy to see. On a dual carriageway they will have an amber flashing light, but on other roads you may not have that advance warning.

Buses and coaches

Look well ahead when you see buses and coaches at a bus stop. Be aware of

- people getting off the bus or coach and not looking properly before they cross the road (even if they look, their view is often restricted)
- buses and coaches pulling away from the bus stop. If they are signalling to move out, always give way to them if you can do so safely.

Pedestrians

When turning from one road to another

- always look out for pedestrians
- give way to any who are crossing
- take extra care if a pedestrian fails to look your way as you approach.

Pedestrian crossings - Never overtake on the approach to pedestrian crossings.

Older people - Several factors make older people more vulnerable.

Poor eyesight or hearing might mean they are not aware of approaching traffic. They might not be able to judge the speed of approaching traffic when crossing the road. Even when they do realise the danger, they may be unable to move quickly, or they may become flustered.

They may also take longer to cross the road. Be patient and do not hurry them by revving your engine or edging forwards.

Disabled pedestrians - Take special care with visually impaired or disabled people.

Remember that a person with hearing difficulty is not easy to identify.

Visually impaired people may carry a white cane or use a guide dog. Those who are deaf and blind may carry a white cane with a red band.

Children - Look out for children, particularly in residential areas and near schools and parks.

Be aware that a school crossing warden may stop you to escort children across a busy road.

Children are impulsive and often unpredictable. Therefore, ride slowly in narrow roads where parked cars obscure your view. Look out for parked ice cream vans. Children are more interested in ice cream than they are in traffic, and they may run into the road unexpectedly.

Animals

Animals are easily frightened by noise and vehicles coming close to them.

You should

- ride slowly and quietly; don't sound the horn
- keep engine speed low; don't rev your engine
- always watch out for animals on unfenced roads.

Give animals as much room as possible.

> **Remember,** always think of the other road user, not just of yourself.

Persons in charge of animals - If someone in charge of animals signals to you to stop, do so and stop your engine.

Guide dogs - A guide dog for a visually handicapped person usually has a distinctive loop type of harness. Remember, the dog is trained to wait if there's a vehicle nearby.

For a person with hearing difficulty, the guide dog may wear a distinctive yellow or burgundy coloured coat or have a distinctive orange lead and collar.

Horse riders - Be particularly careful when approaching horses, especially those ridden by children.

As a motorcyclist you should

- look out for horses being led or ridden on the road
- take extra care and keep your speed down at left-hand bends especially on narrow country roads
- slow down when you see a horse rider on the road.

As you approach a horse rider from behind

- slow down, give them plenty of room and be prepared to stop
- don't sound your horn or rev your engine. Horses can be easily scared by noise and may panic around fast-moving vehicles
- look out for any signals given by the riders and heed a request to slow down or stop.

Always pass wide and slow.

Take special care when meeting what appears to be a riding-school group. Many of the riders might be inexperienced.

Horses are potential hazards and you should take great care when meeting or passing them.

section **eleven**
RIDING ON MOTORWAYS

This section covers

- Riding on motorways
- Motorways signs
- Motorways signals
- Joining a motorway
- Lane discipline
- Overtaking
- Leaving a motorway
- Motorway weather conditio
- Stopping on motorways
- Roadworks

Riding on motorways

Motorways are designed to help traffic move quickly and safely over long distances. They place demands on both the rider and machine that are different from those of other roads. For example, the effect of weather conditions can be exaggerated by higher speeds.

On motorways situations can develop rapidly so you need to be alert and feeling well.

You'll find that you're exposed to wind turbulence, particularly from larger vehicles and you'll need to anticipate the wind effect so that you can keep full control of your machine.

Remember, use the two-second rule and look well ahead. Don't just focus on the vehicle in front.

Because of the higher speeds, it's important that you can be seen easily by other drivers. Wear high-visibility clothing and ride with your headlamp on dipped beam.

Motorways must not be used by pedestrians, cyclists or horse riders. Holders of provisional car and motorcycle licences are also not allowed on motorways.

In addition the following vehicles must not be used on the motorway

- motorcycles under 50 cc
- certain slow-moving vehicles with oversized loads - except with special permission
- most invalid carriages
- agricultural vehicles.

Due to the demanding nature of motorways, make sure that

- you have a thorough knowledge of the sections of the *The Highway Code* dealing with motorways
- you know and understand the motorway warning signs and signals
- you feel fit and alert to ride. Never use the motorway if you feel tired or unwell
- you never park except at service areas. If you need to rest, you'll sometimes have to travel long distances before an exit or a service area. Remember, it's an offence to stop on the hard shoulder, an exit or a slip road, unless in an emergency.

The motorcycle on the motorway

High speeds and long distances increase the risk of mechanical failure. You should carry out the following checks

- tyres - they must be in good condition and with the correct pressure. Follow the guidance given in the owner's handbook which often tells you the different pressures to be used when carrying a passenger or load
- instruments - make sure there are no faults
- warning lights - make sure each is working correctly
- mirrors (if fitted) - make sure they are clean and correctly positioned
- lights and indicators - make sure they are all working correctly.

A quick check before using the motorway might prevent a breakdown during your journey

Also make sure that

- your brakes can stop you safely
- your steering is in good order.

For safety, convenience and good vehicle care you should also check the following items

- fuel - make sure you have enough fuel to avoid running out between service areas
- oil - high speeds may mean your engine uses oil
- water (liquid cooled engines) - higher speeds can mean a warmer engine, especially in traffic tailbacks in hot weather.

Make sure any load is secure - Check that everything carried on your motorcycle or trailer is safe and secure.

If anything should fall from your motorcycle or from another vehicle, stop on the hard shoulder and use the emergency telephone to inform the police. Never try to retrieve it yourself.

Motorway signs

Leading to the motorway

Direction signs from ordinary roads to the motorway have white lettering and figures on a blue panel, often bordered in white.

These signs may stand alone or be included in other larger signs of various colours.

On the motorway

You may find the following types of sign on the motorway

- advance direction signs
- countdown markers
- signs giving information about service areas
- signs with a brown background indicating tourist attractions which can be reached by leaving at the next exit.

All these signs are very much larger than those on ordinary roads because you need to be able to see them from a distance. This is a good reminder that you must leave more room for all manoeuvres when riding on a motorway.

Each junction has an identifying number which corresponds with current road maps, to help you plan your route and know where you need to leave the motorway.

Speed limit signs

Signs which display a speed limit within a red ring indicate mandatory maximum speed limits and are often seen at roadworks or on overhead gantries. You must obey these signs. If you don't, you risk prosecution.

Motorway signals

Signals will warn of dangers ahead, such as accidents, fog and icy roads.

Flashing amber lights

Look out for flashing amber lights and signs either on the central reservation or overhead. These warn you of lane closures, roadworks and other hazards.

They might also show a temporary advisory speed limit, so

- slow down to the speed limit
- be ready to slow down still more to pass the obstacle or danger
- look out for police signs
- don't speed up until you see the sign ending the temporary restriction (or there are no more flashing amber lights).

Red lights

Some signs have flashing red lights as well.

A red light (it may be a red 'X') warns you that you must not go beyond the red light in that lane, so

- start to slow down in good time
- be ready to change lanes.

If the red light flashes on a slip road, you must not enter it.

If a red light flashes on the central reservation or at the side of the road, you must not go beyond the signal in any lane.

Joining a motorway

At an entry point where a slip road leads to the motorway, try to adjust your speed to that of the traffic already on the motorway before joining it.

Give priority to traffic already on the motorway. Join where there's a suitable gap in the left-hand lane.

Use the OSM/PSL routine. A lifesaver glance will verify the position of other vehicles. Try to avoid stopping at the end of the slip road unless queuing to join other slow-moving traffic.

Make sure you

- indicate your intention to join the motorway
- can be seen
- assess the speed of the traffic on the motorway before you try to merge in.

A tapering chevron helps you to gauge the distance to where the slip road joins the motorway

You should avoid forcing your way into the traffic stream or riding along the hard shoulder.

Once you've joined the motorway, keep in the left-hand lane until you've had time to judge and adjust to the speed of the traffic already on the motorway.

In a very few cases, the lane merges from the right. Take extra care when joining or meeting traffic at these locations.

When other vehicles join the motorway

After you pass an exit, there's usually an entrance where other vehicles can join.

- Don't try to race them while they're on the slip road
- Look well ahead if there are several vehicles joining the motorway - be prepared to adjust your speed
- If it's safe, move to another lane to make it easier for joining traffic to merge.

On the motorway

Continually reassess the movement of the vehicles, directly ahead (in the near and far distance), alongside you and behind you.

At high speeds, situations change rapidly. Effective observation helps you prepare for any sudden developments.

For example, an increase in the number of vehicles ahead could mean that traffic is slowing down and 'bunching', or a flashing breakdown light will warn you to slow down until you're sure of what's happening.

If you see serious congestion ahead, you can use hazard warning lights (if fitted) briefly to alert drivers behind you. This can reduce the risk of rear-end collisions, especially in bad weather.

Keeping your distance

The faster the traffic, the more time and space you need.

You must give yourself greater margins than on ordinary roads and make sure there's enough space between you and the vehicle ahead. Traffic normally travels faster because there are usually no

- ordinary junctions
- sharp bends*
- roundabouts*
- steep hills

- traffic lights
- slow moving vehicles.

*Some motorway links, where motorway regulations also apply, have roundabouts and sharp bends.

How big a gap? - Leave a gap of at least one metre or yard for each mph of your speed. A useful method of judging this is to use the two-second rule (see page 114). This rule is reinforced on some motorways where there are chevrons painted on the carriageway. Keep at least two chevrons between you and the vehicle in front.

Adverse weather - Leave at least double the space if the road is wet or slippery.

Obstructions

If vehicles ahead switch on their hazard warning lights be prepared for slow-moving or stationary traffic.

Look well ahead and leave yourself plenty of room. Check behind to see how the traffic behind you is reacting.

If you find yourself catching up with slower moving traffic there could be an obstruction ahead. Be aware that other vehicles may be slowing gradually without the need to brake. You won't have warning from their brake lights in these situations.

Lane discipline

Lane discipline is vitally important on motorways. You should normally ride in the left-hand lane.

- Don't change lanes unless you need to.
- Ride in the centre of the lane.
- Don't wander into another lane.

Changing lanes on a motorway

Always use the OSM/PSL routine well before you intend to change lanes. At higher speeds, you must start the routine much earlier.

Look, and if necessary, signal in good time. Remember vehicles might come up behind very quickly.

The sooner you indicate, the sooner other drivers are warned of your intended movement. They'll expect a change in the traffic pattern and have time to prepare for it.

Two-lane motorways

On a two-lane motorway, the correct position is in the left-hand lane.

The right-hand (offside) lane is for overtaking and once you have overtaken you should return to the left-hand lane as soon as it is safe to do so.

Large goods vehicles are permitted to use either lane.

Motorways with three or four lanes

Because of the volume of traffic on three-lane motorways, many are being widened to four or more lanes in each direction.

Keep to the left-hand lane unless there are a great many slower vehicles ahead.

Avoid repeatedly changing lane – it's possible to stay in the centre or outer lanes while you are overtaking a number of slower moving vehicles, but don't stay in these lanes

- longer than you have to
- if you are delaying traffic behind you.

Drivers of large goods vehicles, buses, coaches or any vehicle towing a trailer are not allowed to use the extreme right-hand lane of a motorway with more than two lanes, unless one or more lanes are temporarily closed.

> **Remember,** the right hand lane is for overtaking - it's not the 'fast lane'

Don't stay in an overtaking lane longer than it takes you to move out, overtake and move in again safely.

Crawler lane

A steep hill on a motorway might have a crawler or climbing lane to avoid heavy vehicles slowing down the flow of traffic.

Crawler lanes help to keep the traffic flowing by providing an extra lane for slow vehicles

Overtaking

Leave a safe distance between you and the vehicle you intend to overtake.

Use the appropriate parts of the OSM/PSL routine. For example

Observation - Check behind to verify the speed, course and position of traffic behind you.

Position - Position yourself so that you can see well past the vehicle in front.

Speed - Make sure you're going fast enough or can accelerate quickly enough to overtake without blocking any vehicle coming up behind.

Look - Look ahead and behind to check if there's anything preventing you from overtaking safely. For example, a lane closure ahead, or traffic coming up much faster from behind in the right-hand lane.

Try to anticipate if the vehicle ahead will move out to overtake.

- Look
- Assess well ahead
- Decide – don't rush
- Act – but only when you're sure it's safe.

Observation - Remember that vehicles coming up in the right-hand lane are likely to be moving faster than you are.

Be on the look out for vehicles returning to the lane you intend to use.

Signal - You must signal well before you start to move out. This gives drivers behind you plenty of time to anticipate what you intend to do and could influence any manoeuvres they're planning.

Pulling out

Take a lifesaver glance into the blind spot before moving out smoothly into an overtaking lane. Cancel your signal and overtake as quickly and safely as possible.

As you overtake a large goods vehicle, bus or coach expect to be buffeted by the changing air pressure. Don't ride too close to the vehicle you're overtaking.

Moving back left

Pass the vehicle and move back into the left as soon as you're sure it's safe to do so.

Don't cut in too soon in front of the vehicle you've just passed.

Look for any vehicles about to move out into the lane you intend to move into.

On busy motorways

If you come up behind traffic moving more slowly than you are when you're overtaking, be patient and don't

- intimidate the driver ahead by repeatedly flashing your headlight and riding dangerously close behind
- filter between fast moving lanes of traffic.

Overtaking on the left

Never overtake on the left, unless

- the traffic is moving in queues and
- the queue on your right is moving more slowly than the queue you are in.

Never use the hard shoulder to overtake - unless directed to do so by traffic signs at road works, or by police officers.

Ride defensively and let faster traffic pass you. Don't move to a lane on the left to overtake

Leaving a motorway

Unless you're going to the end of the motorway, you'll leave by moving left from the left-hand lane into the slip road.

Plan well ahead, particularly on motorways with three or four lanes. Use your mirrors and signal left in good time to move into the left-hand lane.

You should avoid

- moving to the left more than one lane at a time
- cutting across at the last moment, especially from the second lane of a motorway with three or four lanes.

Road signs

Use the road signs and markers to help you time your exit and use your mirrors and indicators appropriately.

You'll have plenty of time to observe the signs and markers so there's no need to rush.

Travelling on a motorway with three or four lanes, could mean changing lanes more than once, and you should follow the OSM routine for each change of lane.

One mile before the exit - A junction sign with road numbers and main destinations on that road, as well as the junction number.

Half a mile before the exit - A sign that repeats the information on the one mile sign.

Countdown markers - These occur at 270 metres (300 yards), 180 metres (200 yards) and 90 metres (100 yards) before the start of the slip road.

At the beginning of the slip road - A sign shows the destinations off the slip road and ahead.

Occasionally, where motorways merge, there may be an exit just prior to the one you intend to take. In these cases, or where there are service areas near to exits, look well ahead for the advance warning signs.

If you miss your exit, carry on to the next exit.

End of motorway

There will be end-of-motorway signs at all exits. These mean that the road you're joining will have different rules.

Remember to watch for any signs telling you what these are, particularly

- speed limits
- dual carriageway
- two-way traffic
- clearway
- motorway link road
- part-time traffic lights.

Speed when leaving a motorway

After riding at motorway speeds for some time, your judgement of speed will almost certainly be affected - 40 or 45 mph seems more like 20 mph.

- Adjust your riding to suit the new conditions.
- Check your speedometer. It will give you the accurate speed.

Motorway slip roads and link roads often have sharp curves which should be taken at much lower speeds. The road surface on these curves may be slippery and look for spilt diesel fuel.

When you leave the motorway it could take you time to adjust to lower speed limits

Motorway weather conditions

When you ride on motorways the most common weather problems will be crosswinds, rain and fog.

Crosswinds

A sudden gust of wind can blow you off course. Keep your speed down where there is a danger of crosswinds.

Remember, in strong wind, drivers of high-sided vehicles, or those towing caravans, are also likely to experience difficulties. Allow for this when riding near these vehicles.

Riding more slowly will help you to keep control. You need to be especially careful as you come out from the shelter of a large vehicle when overtaking or being overtaken especially on exposed stretches.

In severe windy weather some exposed stretches of the motorway are closed for safety reasons. Check with a local radio station or motoring organisation before setting out.

Rain

In heavy rain the surface spray from other vehicles, especially large ones, will seriously reduce visibility, as well as increase stopping distance. Make sure that

- you're visible. Use dipped headlights and wear bright clothing
- you can see clearly. Keep your visor or goggles clean
- you adjust your speed to suit the conditions and leave larger separation distances, at least double the normal.

Fog

In fog you need to

- slow down and keep your distance from the vehicle ahead
- use dipped headlamps and rear fog lamps (if fitted) when visibility falls below 100 metres (about 330 feet)
- make sure that your visor or goggles are clean and aren't hindering your view ahead
- wear bright clothing. This will help other drivers to see you.

Fog can drift quickly and is often patchy. If a motorway warning sign shows 'Fog' be prepared and reduce speed in good time.

Stopping on motorways

Motorway service areas have lane markings and signs to help direct you

You must only stop on a motorway if it's an emergency, such as stopping to prevent an accident or because the police, road signs or signals indicate that you must.

If you need to stop for a rest, find a service area. The hard shoulder is for emergencies only, it isn't for parking or resting.

Breakdowns

If your motorcycle breaks down, try to get onto the hard shoulder. When you have stopped

- park as far to the left as you can away from the traffic
- switch on hazard warning lights if fitted
- switch on your parking lights in poor visibility or at night

- make your way to the nearest emergency telephone and call for assistance. Never attempt even minor repairs.

Emergency telephones - Police-controlled emergency telephones are on most stretches of motorway at one mile intervals.

Remember, never cross the carriageway or an exit or entry slip road to reach a phone or for any other purpose.

Look for a telephone symbol and arrows on marker posts 100 metres (328 feet) apart along the hard shoulder.

The arrow directs you to the nearest phone on your side of the carriageway. Walk to the telephone, keeping on the inside of the hard shoulder.

Using the emergency phone - The telephone connects you to police control, who will put you through to a breakdown service. Always face the traffic when you speak on the telephone.

You'll be asked for

- the number on the telephone, which gives your precise location
- details of your vehicle and your membership details, if you belong to one of the motoring organisations
- details of the fault.

If you're a vulnerable motorcyclist such as a woman travelling alone, make this clear to the operator.

You'll also be told approximately how long you'll have to wait.

Mobile phones - If you are unable to use an emergency telephone, use a mobile phone if you have one. Before you call, make sure that you can give the police precise details of your location. Marker posts on the side of the hard shoulder identify your location and you should provide these details when you call.

Waiting for the emergency services

Many motorway deaths are caused by vehicles driving into people on the hard shoulder. For this reason wait on the bank near your vehicle, so you can see the emergency services arriving.

Rejoining the motorway

Don't pull straight out onto the carriageway. Use the hard shoulder as an acceleration lane to build up speed before joining the left-hand lane when there's a gap.

Face the traffic when using an emergency telephone

Roadworks

Accidents can often happen at roadworks when drivers fail to observe simple rules of safety. So

- reduce speed in good time when warned by the advance warning signs or flashing signals
- get into the lane indicated for use by your vehicle in good time
- obey all speed limits
- keep the correct separation distance from the vehicle ahead
- avoid sharp braking and sudden changes of direction
- don't change lanes when signs tell you to stay in your lane
- don't let your concentration wander
- don't speed up until you're clear of the roadworks.

Contraflow systems

These are temporary systems where traffic travelling in opposite directions shares the same carriageway. They allow traffic to keep moving during repairs or alterations on the other carriageway.

While contraflow systems are usually found on motorways, they may also be used on other roads carrying fast-moving traffic.

At the start and end of a contraflow system, rows of cones guide the streams of traffic. Once in a contraflow, the lanes are often narrower than normal lanes. Red and white marker posts separate traffic travelling in opposite directions and fluorescent or reflective bright green/yellow studs often replace normal ones.

Watch out for

- lane change signs
- vehicles broken down ahead. There's often no hard shoulder
- vehicles braking ahead – keep your distance.

Mobile roadworks

Minor maintenance work may sometimes be carried out without the need for major lane closures. Slow moving or stationary works vehicles, with a large arrow on the back of the vehicle, are used to divert traffic to the right or left as appropriate.

There may be no cones or other delineators when these vehicles are being used.

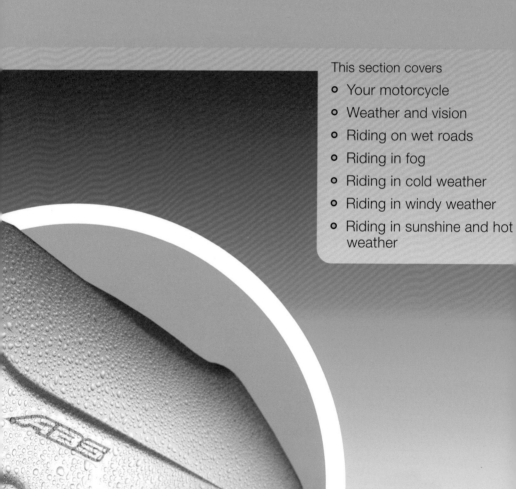

section **twelve**
RIDING IN BAD WEATHER

This section covers

- Your motorcycle
- Weather and vision
- Riding on wet roads
- Riding in fog
- Riding in cold weather
- Riding in windy weather
- Riding in sunshine and hot weather

Your motorcycle

Whatever the weather, make sure your motorcycle is in good condition and regularly checked and serviced. Contending with the elements can be difficult but having to contend with a poorly performing motorcycle at the same time is an extra difficulty you should avoid.

Tyres

Be prepared - don't wait until the bad weather before checking your tyres.

Check for

- tread depth
- pressure
- objects stuck in the tyre
- cuts or damage.

Your safety could depend on a few millimetres of rubber which should have been there. Incorrect tyre pressures can cause loss of stability, reduced grip and increased wear.

Brakes

Keep your brakes in good condition. Wet weather will increase your stopping distance even with perfect brakes.

Electrics

Motorcycle electrical systems are exposed to the elements. Damp or wet affecting your ignition systems can cause

- starting problems
- the engine to misfire. A misfiring engine will cause loss of power and may stop running altogether.

Keep your battery in good condition. In cold weather an electric starter places big demands on the battery.

Lights

Always keep your lights and indicators clean and check for faulty bulbs. Dirty lights can seriously reduce how far you can see and how well other people can see you and your signals.

Weather and vision

The biggest single danger to any rider is being unable to see properly. You won't be able to make the right decisions if you can't see the road clearly.

Rain

Heavy rain on your visor or goggles can affect your view of the road. If you can't see clearly, stop and demist your visor or goggles. It's a good idea to carry a cloth with you especially for this purpose.

If you wear glasses it may be that they too have misted over. Don't be tempted to ride without your glasses if you need them to bring your eyesight up to the legal requirement.

Some modern helmets have air vents to help prevent fogging up and anti-fog products are also available.

Keeping dry - If you allow yourself to get wet you'll also get cold. Being cold and wet can seriously reduce your ability to concentrate.

Proper motorcycle clothing is available which will keep you dry in the heaviest downpour. Good motorcycle clothing is a must if you intend to ride in bad weather.

Fog

When riding in fog you may have the combined problems of

- fogging up on the inside of visors or goggles, and
- misting over on the outside of visors or goggles.

Water droplets can form evenly across the outside of your visor or goggles. This can be difficult to detect since it appears the loss of vision is being caused by the density of the fog rather than this mist of water droplets. Frequently wipe your visor or goggles to prevent this mist obscuring your view of the road.

In freezing fog the mist build up can quickly freeze over. Once frozen you will have to stop and de-ice your visor or goggles to restore a clear view.

Being seen

Making yourself visible to other road users is important at all times. In the rain and fog it's especially so, because of the reduction in visibility.

Wear bright, high visibility clothing and keep your headlamp on dipped beam.

Riding on wet roads

Wet roads reduce tyre grip. Give yourself plenty of time and room for slowing down and stopping. Keep well back from other vehicles.

On a wet road, you should allow at least double the braking distance for a dry road.

After a spell of dry weather, rain on the road can make the surface even more slippery. Take extra care, especially when cornering.

Be aware that different road surfaces might affect the grip of your tyres.

Surface water

When the rain is very heavy or if the road has poor drainage you'll have to deal with surface water.

If you ride too fast through surface water your tyres might not be able to displace water quickly enough. A thin film of water can then build up between the tyre and the road so that the tyre loses contact with the road and all grip is lost. The effect is called 'aquaplaning'. High speed and worn tyres increase the risk of aquaplaning.

To avoid aquaplaning

• keep your speed down
• avoid riding through water pooling on the road surface – if you can do so safely.

If you feel your motorcycle start to aquaplane ease off the throttle. Don't brake or turn the steering until grip is restored.

Try not to splash pedestrians by riding through pools of water close to the kerb.

Heavy rain and surface water make it easier for skidding to occur and make aquaplaning a possibility

191

Brakes

As well as reducing tyre grip water can also reduce the effectiveness of your brakes and you'll need a longer distance to stop. You should allow for this and keep your speed down.

If the surface is good but wet, you should

- aim to brake when the machine is in its most stable position, that is, upright and moving straight ahead
- apply the front brake slightly before the rear. Spread the braking effort evenly between the front and rear brakes.

Motorcyclists need to be aware of slippery surfaces caused by rain on

- metal drain covers
- muddy roads and leaves
- painted road markings
- fuel spillages. This may appear as a rainbow coloured film on the road surface.

These surfaces need extra care when cornering or braking.

Floods

Before you ride through flood water stop and assess how deep the water is. Roads that flood regularly may have depth gauges. You can check the depth on these.

If the water seems too deep turn back and go around the flood by another route. It may take a little longer but it's better than becoming stranded in the flood.

If the water is not too deep, ride through slowly and

- keep in a low gear
- keep your engine running fast enough to prevent water entering the exhaust
- try to ride where the water is most shallow. Due to camber on roads this is likely to be in the crown of the road. Watch for oncoming vehicles who may be doing the same thing
- test your brakes when you're out of the water.

Crossing fords

A ford is a place where a stream crosses a road and so the road surface is also a stream bed. It may

- be very uneven with loose stones
- have a slippery coating over many of the surfaces
- have a strong current.

This can all make riding through a ford a very hazardous activity.

The depth of water at fords varies with the weather and is usually greater in winter.

There may be a depth gauge.

If the water is not too deep for your motorcycle, cross using the same technique as you would for a flood. Remember to test your brakes after you cross. There might be a notice reminding you to do so.

Don't try to displace the water by charging at it. This may cause

- your motorcycle to stall
- you to lose control resulting in falling off, injury to yourself, your passenger or another road user and maybe even damage to property
- you to end up blocking the road.

Riding in fog

Fog is one of the most dangerous weather conditions.

An accident involving one vehicle can quickly involve many others, especially if they're travelling too close to one another.

Motorway pile-ups in fog have sometimes involved dozens of vehicles.

> **Remember,** if the fog is very thick and you can see the rear lights of the vehicle ahead then ask yourself 'Could I stop in an emergency without running into the vehicle in front'

All too often, there's a loss of life or serious injury, which could so easily be prevented.

Observe the obvious

You don't need a sign to tell you it's foggy if you can only see a short distance ahead!

Avoid riding in fog

Take alternative transport or postpone your journey, if at all possible.

If you must make the journey, give yourself time to prepare, check all lights, clean your visor or goggles, and so on. Allow more time for the journey.

Fog patches

The density of fog varies. Sometimes the fog is patchy. One moment it can be fairly clear, the next extremely dense. Avoid the temptation to speed up between patches.

Use of lights

When riding in fog in daylight, you must use your dipped headlight when visibility is seriously reduced because it'll be seen from a much greater distance than sidelights.

Don't use main beam when you're in fog because

- the fog reflects the light and can dazzle you, reducing your view even further
- you can dazzle other drivers.

High-intensity rear fog light - If your motorcycle has a high-intensity rear fog light, use it only in fog when visibility is less than 100 metres (328 feet).

You must switch it off when visibility improves – it is the law. Using it at other times, such as in the rain, can dazzle drivers behind you.

Adjust your lights - Change your lighting with the conditions.

For example, when you're queuing in traffic and the driver behind has already seen you, it can be helpful to switch off your rear fog lights temporarily to avoid dazzle.

Visibility

Poor visibility is frustrating and puts a strain on the eyes. Your ability to anticipate is dangerously restricted.

It's also much more difficult to judge distances and speed in fog when outlines become confusing. You can easily become disoriented – especially on an unfamiliar road.

If you find yourself in fog

- slow down so that you can stop within your range of vision
- use your dipped headlight
- keep your visor or goggles clear
- keep your distance from the vehicle in front
- use your rear fog lamp (if fitted) when visibility falls below 100 metres (about 330 feet).

Positioning

Try to keep a central position between lane lines or studs.

Don't mix up lane lines and centre lines.

Riding too close to the centre could mean you're dangerously near someone coming the other way doing the same thing.

Riding on the centre line as a means of finding your way is extremely dangerous.

Don't ride in the gutter as parked vehicles, cyclists and pedestrians could appear suddenly.

Following another vehicle

Slow down and leave plenty of room for stopping.

There may be something ahead which you cannot possibly see until you're close to it.

If the vehicle ahead has to stop suddenly, you must have ample time to react and brake.

You may not see or recognise that the vehicle ahead is braking, or has stopped, as soon as you would in clear weather.

You need to be able to brake safely, so remember the road surface is often slippery in fog.

Overtaking

Overtaking in fog can be particularly dangerous. Never begin to overtake unless you can clearly see that it's safe to do so. There won't be many such opportunities when riding in mist or fog. You could well find that visibility ahead is much worse than you thought, and you won't be able to see oncoming traffic soon enough.

Junctions in fog

Dealing with junctions in fog needs particular care, especially when turning right. Traffic will generally be moving more slowly and may be difficult to hear.

When dealing with a foggy junction you should

- listen for approaching traffic
- start indicating as early as you can
- make the greatest possible use of your lights. If you keep your foot on the brake pedal while you're stopped, your brake lights will give drivers behind an extra warning
- use the horn if you feel it will help.

Don't turn until you're absolutely sure it's safe.

Road markings

Dipped headlights will pick out reflective studs, but it's not so easy to recognise other road markings when driving in fog. Explanations of the different coloured studs are given on page 88.

Parking in fog

Never park on a road in the fog if you can avoid it. Find an off-street parking place.

However, if it is unavoidable, always leave your parking lights on.

Breaking down

If you break down, get your motorcycle off the road if you possibly can.

Inform the police, and make arrangements to remove it as soon as possible if it creates an obstruction.

Never leave it without warning lights of some kind or on the wrong side of the road.

Riding in cold weather

Stop to warm up before you lose feeling in your fingers. You won't be able to operate the controls properly if your fingers become numb

If you get cold when riding

- your concentration will suffer
- your ability to control your machine will be affected
- your enjoyment of motorcycling will be lessened.

Keeping warm can be a problem. There is motorcycle clothing available which will keep you warm in very low temperatures. This clothing isn't cheap, but it's essential if you want to ride in cold weather.

The cold will probably affect your hands and feet first. Don't continue if you lose feeling in your fingers or toes. Stop now and then to warm up.

Snow and ice

It's better not to ride at all in conditions of snow and ice. If you must travel in these conditions keep to the main roads. These are more likely to be clear and well gritted.

When riding on snow or ice your tyres have reduced grip on the road. Keep your speed down and take great care when

- accelerating
- braking
- cornering.

Snow

In falling snow, use your dipped headlight and keep your visor or goggles clear. Snow will quickly cover road signs and markings. Be aware of the danger this creates.

Snow can also build up over your headlight and front indicators as you ride. This will quickly reduce their effectiveness. If this happens stop frequently to clear the snow away.

Ice

Overnight freezing usually results in an icy surface, especially on less used roads. Look for signs of frost on verges, etc.

It's even more dangerous when the roads are just beginning to freeze or thaw. The combination of water and ice adds up to an extremely slippery surface.

You need to watch for areas where ice may linger after it's cleared elsewhere. This may be

- areas of shade caused by features such as trees, hedges, and buildings
- exposed roads where wind chill keeps the ground temperature low
- low lying areas where cold air gathers
- shaded hills and slopes.

Other road users may not appreciate how severely the conditions are affecting you. If someone is following too closely, pull over and let them go past.

If your machine is left out overnight and it's covered in frost or ice in the morning this is an obvious clue that the roads may also be affected

Black ice

Black ice is very dangerous. It forms when droplets of water freeze on a normally good skid resistant surface. Black ice is so dangerous because it's almost invisible.

In wintry conditions, if the road looks wet but you can't hear tyre noise as you would on a wet road, suspect black ice.

A strong gust of wind from your left could blow you towards oncoming traffic

Riding in windy weather

A strong gust of wind from one side can suddenly blow you off course. You're likely to be affected by these crosswinds

- as you pass gateways or gaps in hedges
- as you pass gaps in buildings
- as you pass high-sided vehicles
- on exposed roads.

When it's windy keep your speed down so that you can remain in control. Look ahead and anticipate places where crosswinds may affect you.

Crosswinds can affect other road users too. These include

- cyclists
- high-sided vehicles
- vehicles towing trailers or caravans.

Riding in sunshine and hot weather

Motorcycling is probably at its best during warm, dry weather.

Clear visor/goggles

There are generally more flies and insects about in hot weather, and they can soon cause a dirty and smeary visor or goggles.

This can reduce your view of the road, especially at night and worsen the effects of glare.

Always keep your visor or goggles clean and free from smears (see page 43).

Dust and dirt can cause tiny scratches on visors and goggles. These scratches build up over time. Replace your visor or goggles if they become heavily scratched.

Clothing

Never be tempted to ride without wearing protective clothing, even on the hottest days. You could be horribly injured from even the most minor accident.

Glare

Constant sun in your eyes can be exhausting on a long journey and may well affect your concentration.

Even if you don't feel the need, the correct sunglasses can help reduce glare and ease the strain on your eyes.

This is especially important if you're riding abroad, where conditions are hotter and the sunlight brighter than you may be used to.

If the roads are wet, reflected glare seriously reduces your ability to see. Reduce speed and take extra care.

Low-angle sun

Glare can be worse in the winter when the sun is low in the sky. Wearing sunglasses or using an approved tinted visor can help to reduce the glare. If you're affected, slow down so that you can stop within the distance you can see. Avoid looking directly into the sun.

You must not wear tinted glasses, visors or goggles in the dark and during conditions of poor visibility.

Low sun both dazzles and casts long shadows that can conceal hazards

Road surface

During a long hot, dry spell the road surface will become coated with rubber, particularly at

- junctions
- bends
- roundabouts.

When it rains after such a dry spell the road will be unusually slippery. Look out for shiny surfaces.

If you park on soft tarmac the stand can sink into the road surface

Loose chippings

Many highway authorities replace the granite chipping road surfaces during the summer. While this work is being carried out you may have to ride on temporary road surfaces. These can be very rough and watch for humps at the beginning and end of the temporary surface. You should

- take extra care
- observe the special warning speed limits
- keep well back from the vehicle in front.

When a road has been resurfaced with chippings it has a very loose surface for several days. Loose chippings will reduce your tyres' grip on the road. When riding on loose chippings, take care when

- accelerating
- braking
- cornering.

Watch for the warning signs and reduced speed limits.

Flying stone chips can cause

- expensive damage to your vehicle
- eye injury if you ride without wearing goggles or with your visor raised
- serious injury to pedestrians and other road users.

Soft tarmac

During long periods of hot weather, many tarmac road surfaces become extremely soft. Take care braking and cornering. Melted tar can reduce tyre grip and lead to skidding.

section **thirteen**
RIDING AT NIGHT

This section covers

- Seeing at night
- Lights
- Being seen
- Built up areas
- Overtaking or following at night
- Parking at night
- Meeting other vehicles

Seeing at night

Riding at night is another aspect of motorcycling which demands special techniques and precautions.

You should have your eyesight checked regularly.

Ask yourself, 'Can I really see as well as I would like?'

If you can't see so well at night, it might be your eyes that are to blame; night riding may be highlighting the need for an eyesight check.

Make sure you can stop within the distance lit up by your headlamp

How far can you see?

Test yourself in a suitable place.

Pick an object within the range of your lights and see if you can stop by the time you reach it.

> **Remember,** when you leave a brightly lit service area, your eyes will need time to adjust to the darkness.

You'll be surprised how difficult this is with dipped lights on an unlit road, and shows that you should take a good look before you dip your lights.

Adjusting to darkness

Give your eyes a minute or two to adjust to the darkness, particularly when you're coming out of a brightly lit area or building.

To help you see at night you should keep your goggles or visor clean. Scratches on either can cause dazzle from approaching traffic. If your goggles or visor become scratched you should replace them.

If you're riding in the dark don't wear

- sunglasses
- tinted goggles
- a tinted visor.

Lights

To help other road users to see you, ride with your headlight on dipped beam at all times – even in good daylight.

At night, your vehicle lights are the most important source of information for both you and for other road users.

- Keep your lights clean.
- Check all your lights before any journey.
- Fix any lighting fault immediately, for your own safety, and the safety of others. Carry spare bulbs.
- Practise operating the light switches so that you can find them easily in the dark.
- Remember that extra weight of a pillion passenger or a load could cause your headlight to aim higher than normal. This could cause dazzle to other road users and reduced the effectiveness of your headlight. Adjust your headlight to deal with this.

Using dipped beam

You must use a dipped headlight

- at night when street lighting is poor, for example if street lights are more than 185 metres (600 feet) apart
- in poor visibility
- at night on all other roads including motorways.

Using main beam

Use your headlight on main beam in any conditions where the main beam will help you to see without dazzling other road users.

When your headlight is on main beam the blue main beam warning lamp will glow.

Dipping your headlight - Dip your main beam

- in the face of oncoming traffic
- when approaching traffic from behind.

Don't dazzle other road users – you could cause an accident.

When you dip your headlight

- you'll see less of the road ahead
- slow down so that you can stop within the distance you can see.

Being seen

At night it's more difficult for other road users to see you in good time. In congested urban areas a single motorcycle headlight can get lost in the background of distracting lights.

Although bright fluorescent clothing is highly effective at increasing your visibility in daylight it is less effective in the dark when reflective material should be used. Reflective material works by reflecting light shone onto it, such as headlamps, and this helps to make it easier for others to see you at night.

Reflective material can be worn such as

- reflective strips or panels integrated into motorcycle clothing
- hi-visibility safety overjackets or tabards
- Sam Browne belt.

Reflectors are fitted to all motorcycles by manufacturers and you should make sure they are clean. You may also fit additional reflective panels or tape to further increase your visibility.

Be aware of the difficulty other road users might have and

- ride with dipped beam, unless you need to use the full beam
- keep your lamps clean and working correctly
- keep your reflective number plate clean.

Wearing bright clothing with reflective panels makes it easier for others to see you, especially from the side such as here at a road junction

The bright lights in a busy street can be distracting and make it difficult to see hazards that are poorly lit

Built-up areas

Always use dipped beam in built-up areas at night. It helps others to see you!

In areas where street lights cause patches of shadow, watch out for pedestrians, especially those in dark clothes, who can be difficult to see.

Remember

- be on the alert for pedestrians
- approach pedestrian crossings at a speed at which you can stop safely if necessary
- watch for cyclists and joggers.

Noise at night

Keep all noise to a minimum and try not to disturb residents who may be asleep.

- Don't rev your engine unnecessarily.
- Take extra care setting or disarming any anti-theft alarm on your motorcycle.

Using the horn at night - You must not use your horn between 11.30 pm and 7 am in a built-up area (except to avoid danger from a moving vehicle).

If you need to warn other road users of your presence at night, flash your headlight.

Overtaking or following at night

You'll need to take extra care before attempting to overtake at night. It's more difficult because you can see less.

Only overtake if you can see that the road ahead will remain clear until after you have finished the manoeuvre. Don't overtake if there's a chance you are approaching

- a road junction or bend
- the brow of a bridge or hill, except on a dual carriageway
- a pedestrian crossing
- double white lines

or if there's likely to be a vehicle overtaking or turning right or any other potential hazard.

Stay clear and dip

Make sure you don't get too close to the vehicle ahead, and always dip your headlight so you don't cause dazzle.

Your light beam should fall short of the rear of the vehicle in front.

Remember your separation distance.

On a dual carriageway or motorway where it's possible to overtake, don't use full beam in the face of oncoming drivers.

If you're being overtaken

Dip your headlight as soon as the vehicle passes you.

Don't dazzle the driver in front. Hold back so that your headlamp beam falls short of their vehicle

Parking at night

Cars, light goods vehicles (1525 kg or less unladen) and motorcycles can park without lights on roads with a speed limit of 30 mph or less. They must comply with any parking restrictions, and not park within 10 metres (32 feet) of a junction.

They must also be parked parallel to, and close to, the side of the road or in a designated parking place and facing in the direction of the traffic flow.

Always switch your headlight off when you stop, even for a short while. It's an offence to leave it on when parked. The fixed glare can be very dazzling, especially if, for any reason, you've parked on the offside of the road facing oncoming traffic.

Never leave your motorcycle on any other road without using the parking lights unless a sign indicates that lights are not required; it's better to get it off the road altogether.

Also avoid leaving your motorcycle standing on the right-hand side of the road, except in a one-way street.

To deter thieves it's a good idea to park in a well-lit area at night and using some form of an alarm can also help

Meeting other vehicles

Another vehicle's lights can tell you which direction they're heading and can give you an idea of their speed. Oncoming lights should raise a number of questions in your mind, such as

- how far away is the vehicle and how fast is it moving?
- should I slow down while we pass each other?
- how soon should I dip my headlight?
- how far ahead can I see before I dip?
- before I dip, is there anything on my side of the road that I might endanger or that might endanger me? For example, a stationary vehicle, a cyclist, a pedestrian, or an unlit obstacle.

Headlight on full beam

When your headlight is on full beam

- dip early enough to avoid dazzling oncoming drivers, but not too early
- check the left-hand verge before you dip.

When you're dazzled

If the headlights of oncoming vehicles dazzle you, slow down and, if necessary, stop.

You're more likely to be dazzled by the lights of an oncoming vehicle on a right hand bend or on the crest of a hill

Don't look directly at oncoming headlights and don't retaliate by leaving your headlight on full beam and dazzling the oncoming driver.

On a left-hand bend - Dip earlier. Your headlight will point directly towards the eyes of anyone coming toward you as you ride around the bend.

On a right-hand bend - Your headlamp will point at the left edge of the road but approaching traffic's lights will be more likely to dazzle you.

section **fourteen**
PASSENGERS AND LOADS

This section covers

- Carrying a passenger
- Carrying a load
- Sidecar outfits
- Towing a trailer

Carrying a passenger

Riding with a passenger or a load can call for adjustments to your machine as well as your riding.

You must not carry a pillion passenger or pull a trailer unless you have a full motorcycle licence.

Legal requirements

Before you can carry a passenger you must comply with the law.

You're allowed to carry a pillion passenger only if

- you've passed your practical motorcycle test
- you hold a full motorcycle licence for the category of machine you're riding.

To carry a passenger your motorcycle should have

- rear footrests
- a proper passenger seat.

Motorcycle adjustments

To cope with the extra load of a pillion passenger you should

- inflate the tyres according to the maker's instructions
- adjust the pre-load on the rear shock absorbers to allow for the extra weight (see your owner's handbook for details)
- adjust the headlamp aim, if necessary.

Passengers

If your passenger has never ridden pillion before, or you doubt their experience, instruct them to

- sit astride the machine facing forwards
- wear an approved motorcycle helmet, properly fastened
- keep both feet on the passenger footrests until dismounting
- keep a light but firm hold on your waist or the passenger grab handle (if fitted)
- lean with you while going around bends or corners.

Instruct your passenger not to

- look behind or signal for you
- lean to the side to see ahead. This might affect your balance and stability.

Passenger's clothing - Your passenger's clothing should be

- weatherproof and protective
- bright and, if riding at night, reflective.

Don't allow your passenger to wear a scarf or belt loosely fastened. These can get tangled in the wheel or drive chain and cause serious injury.

Riding techniques

Until you get used to carrying a passenger, ride with extra care. The passenger will affect

- your balance, especially at low speeds
- your ability to stop. The extra weight may increase your stopping distance. Allow a bigger gap when following another vehicle
- your acceleration. You'll be slower getting moving so allow more room when emerging at junctions.

Don't

- carry children on a motorcycle unless they can safely use the footrests and handholds and they are wearing a properly fitting helmet
- ask your passenger to look behind or signal for you
- accept any road or traffic information from your passenger without verifying it.

Carrying a load

All riders are allowed to carry loads and there are various methods including panniers, top box, tank bags and luggage racks.

Panniers

There are two types of panniers available; rigidly fixed and throw-over saddlebag.

Whichever type you use, always make sure that you load them evenly. Uneven loading can lead to loss of stability.

Top box

A top box is fastened onto a rack behind the seat. It's easy and quick to use but has its limitations. The weight is carried high up and at the very back of the machine. Don't carry heavy loads in a top box because this can

• reduce stability
• cause low-speed wobble
• cause high-speed weave.

Tank bag

A tank bag is fastened on top of the fuel tank (or dummy tank) and can carry large loads. Take care that the tank bag doesn't interfere with your ability to steer.

Luggage rack

Make sure that any items strapped onto the luggage rack are securely fastened. A loose load could become tangled in the rear wheel and cause an accident.

Adjusting your motorcycle

Make any necessary adjustments to the suspension, tyres and lights.

When riding with a load give yourself the chance to get used to the extra weight. If the load is unevenly distributed and your machine is unbalanced stop and rearrange the load.

215

Sidecar outfits

Motorcycles and sidecar outfits need a very different technique from solo motorcycles

If you want to fit a sidecar you should

- ask your dealer if your machine is suitable
- make sure that, after fitting, the sidecar is fixed correctly to the mounting points
- fit it on the left-hand side of the machine if the machine was registered on or after 1 August 1981.

Aligning the sidecar

Make sure that the motorcycle and sidecar are correctly aligned. If they aren't the outfit will be difficult to control and probably dangerous.

Driving techniques

You must adopt a different technique when driving a motorcycle with a sidecar. Keep your speed down until you've become used to the outfit.

On bends and when turning, the sidecar outfit must be steered because you can't lean the machine over. This requires a deliberate push or pull on the handlebar.

On left-hand bends the sidecar wheel will tend to lift as the weight is thrown outwards. This calls for special care and control.

Braking

Unless a brake is fitted to the sidecar wheel the outfit will tend to pull to the right under heavy braking.

The extra weight of the sidecar may increase the overall stopping distance.

Towing a trailer

You can only tow a trailer behind your motorcycle if

- you have a full motorcycle licence
- your machine has an engine capacity exceeding 125 cc
- the trailer doesn't exceed 1 metre (just over 3 feet) in width
- the distance between the rear axle of the motorcycle and the rear of the trailer is less than 2.5 metres (about 8 feet)
- the motorcycle is clearly marked with its kerbside weight
- the trailer is clearly marked with its unladen weight
- the laden weight of the trailer doesn't exceed 150 kg or two thirds of the kerbside weight of the motorcycle, whichever is less.

You can't tow

- more than one trailer
- a trailer carrying a passenger.

When you tow a trailer remember that

- you must obey the speed limit restrictions which apply for all vehicles towing trailers
- your stopping distance may be increased
- any load in the trailer must be secure
- the trailer must be fitted to the machine correctly.

Don't forget it's there!

section **fifteen**

BASIC MAINTENANCE

This section covers

- Regular checks
- Engine
- Suspension and steering
- Controls
- Electrical systems

Regular checks

A motorcycle needs routine maintenance to keep it in a roadworthy condition. Learning how to carry out routine maintenance yourself will save you time and money.

Many routine maintenance jobs are straightforward and explained in the owner's handbook. More difficult tasks may need to be referred to your dealer. Rider training courses may include some mechanical instructions and advice on maintenance.

You should check the following items on a regular basis:

Engine

- fuel
- oil (engine, gearbox and final drive)
- coolant (liquid cooled engines)
- air filter.

Suspension and steering

- suspension
- steering head bearings
- wheels
- tyres.

Controls

- brakes
- clutch
- throttle.

Electrical systems

- battery
- lights
- horn
- indicators.

Engine

A properly maintained engine will

- start more easily
- use less fuel
- be more reliable
- give optimum performance
- have lower exhaust emissions.

Items that will affect the engine performance include

- spark plugs
- ignition settings
- air filter
- carburettor settings
- valve clearances.

If you aren't confident in your ability to maintain your engine, entrust the work to your dealer.

Fuel

Many modern motorcycles are fitted with fuel gauges and low fuel level warning lamps which flash when petrol levels are low.

If your motorcycle doesn't have a fuel gauge you'll have to remove the filler cap to check how much fuel you have.

Some motorcycles have a reserve supply of petrol which is accessed by setting the petrol tap to a reserve position.

The amount of petrol held in this reserve varies with makes and models but typically may be enough to ride 20 – 30 miles.

When the main tank becomes empty the engine will lose power, and it may cough or even cut out altogether. The petrol tap needs to be moved into the reserve position and there may be a slight lag before the fuel reaches the engine. This could be hazardous in certain circumstances, and it is advisable to refuel before the reserve level is reached.

If you use the reserve, remember to turn the petrol tap off reserve and back to the normal on position when you refuel.

For motorcycles that don't have a fuel gauge it's a good idea to reset the trip meter when you refuel. You can use the mileage to work out when you need to refuel again.

Motorcycle engines - Two types of petrol engines are fitted to motorcycles

- two-stroke engines
- four-stroke engines.

If you don't know which type of engine is fitted to your motorcycle, check the owner's manual or ask your dealer.

Two-stroke engines - The two-stroke engine runs on a combined petrol/oil mixture. A special two-stroke oil needs to be combined with the petrol in a ratio determined by the manufacturer. This may be 20:1, for example. Two-stroke oil is combined with the petrol by either

- directly adding the oil to the petrol when refuelling
- adding two-stroke oil to a special oil tank. The oil is then automatically mixed with the petrol as it is fed into the engine.

When refuelling a motorcycle with a two-stroke engine you must remember to add/check two-stroke oil.

Four-stroke engine - It's important that you use the correct grade of petrol for your engine. Most modern four-stroke motorcycle engines run on unleaded fuel but older models may require lead replacement petrol. Check with your dealer/manufacturer if you aren't sure, or check with an oil company's technical department if you are running an older motorcycle.

Catalytic converter - Leaded or lead replacement fuel must not be used on a motorcycle fitted with a catalytic converter. Even one tankful can permanently damage the system.

Oil

Oil is necessary to lubricate your engine. You need to keep the oil at the level recommended by the vehicle manufacturer.

Check regularly and top up the oil when necessary, especially before a long journey.

How to check the oil level - Your motorcycle will have either

- a dipstick
- a sightglass

to tell you the amount of oil in the engine. See the owner's handbook.

Checking the oil while the engine is cold will give a more accurate result. You should also ensure the vehicle is on a level area and upright. Use the centre stand if your motorcycle is fitted with one.

Motorcycles with a sightglass - You may need a cloth to wipe the sightglass clean. The oil level should be between the 'max' and 'min' marks. If the level is too low top it up to the correct level using the manufacturer's recommended grade of oil.

Motorcycles with a dipstick - Remove the dipstick and wipe it clean. Return it fully into the dipstick opening and then remove it again and look to see the oil level. If the level is too low, top it up to the correct level using the manufacturer's recommended grade of oil.

Oil changes - Observe the manufacturer's recommendations. If a large number of short journeys are involved, change the oil at more frequent intervals, especially in dusty conditions. Remember to have the oil filter changed at the same time.

Oil use - The amount of oil an engine will use depends on the type of engine and the amount of wear as well as how you ride.

You shouldn't

- run the engine when the oil level is below the minimum mark
- add so much oil that the level rises above the maximum mark. You'll create excess pressure that could damage the engine seals and gaskets, and cause oil leaks.

Warning light - If the oil pressure warning light on your instrument panel comes on when you're riding, stop as soon as you can and check the oil level.

Remember, oil is toxic and can cause skin problems. Wash it off your hands immediately.

Keep containers storing oil out of reach of children

Engine lubricating oils - The oil in your engine has to perform several tasks at high pressures and temperatures up to 300° C. It helps to

- resist wear on the moving surfaces
- combat the corrosive acids formed as the hydrocarbons in the fuels are burnt in the engine
- keep the engine cool.

It also has to withstand gradual contamination from both fuel and dirt.

Make sure you always use the lubricants recommended in the handbook.

Gearbox lubricating oils - Most motorcycles use the engine oil to lubricate the gearbox. A few, however, have a separate lubricating oil supply for the gearbox.

This oil is especially formulated for use in the gearbox and you should always follow the instructions in the vehicle handbook.

It's not necessary to drain the gearbox in most cases, but the level should be checked at service intervals.

Shaft final drive lubricating oils - Motorcycles with a shaft final drive have a separate supply held in the final drive housing on the rear wheel hub.

There's a filler/level hole on the housing. Remember to have the motorcycle upright when checking the final drive oil level.

It's important that the correct hypoid-type EP (extreme pressure) oil specified in the vehicle handbook is used.

You may have to squeeze the top-up oil using a plastic bottle and tube.

Chain final drive lubricating oils - Final drive chains wear and require frequent lubrication and adjustment. Special motorcycle chain lubricants are available for this purpose. Allowing your drive chain to run dry will greatly increase the rate of wear.

The drive chain needs to be adjusted until the free play is as specified in the handbook.

When you've adjusted the chain tension you need to check the rear wheel alignment. Marks by the chain adjusters may be provided to make this easy.

If the chain is worn or slack it can jump off the sprocket and lock the rear wheel.

Coolant

Many motorcycle engines are liquid cooled using a mixture of water and anti-freeze. The anti-freeze contains a corrosion inhibitor which reduces rust and prolongs the life of the system. In cold weather, maintain the recommended strength of anti-freeze and have it checked annually.

> **Remember,** never remove a radiator cap when the engine is hot and never add cold water to an overheated engine.

You should frequently check the coolant level, particularly before a long trip, topping up with coolant as necessary. The need to top up often might indicate a leak or other fault in the cooling system; have it checked by your garage/dealer.

Air filter

Replace the air filter at the intervals recommended by the manufacturer, or sooner if the vehicle is used in exceptionally dusty conditions.

Suspension and steering

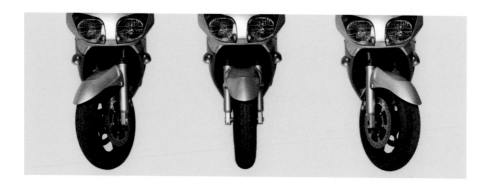

There are several different types of suspension fitted to motorcycles. These range from simple systems with no adjustment to sophisticated systems adjustable for

- preload
- compression
- rebound.

Check your shock absorbers for oil leaks. A faulty oil seal will allow the damping oil to leak out and this can

- make the motorcycle difficult to control
- increase your stopping distance.

There is also a danger that oil leaking from the front forks or a faulty shock absorber may find its way onto the wheel, tyre and brake disc or drum.

Steering head bearings

Steering head bearings allow smooth steering movement. The bearings need to be checked for wear and correct adjustment. Badly adjusted or worn steering head bearings can make the motorcycle difficult to control and may lead to weaving and wobbling.

Steering movement

The handlebars should be free to move from full left lock to full right lock without

- any control cables being stretched, trapped or pinched
- any snagging between moving and fixed parts.

Wheels

Motorcycles are fitted with

- spoked wheels
- alloy wheels
- pressed steel wheels (small-wheeled machines only).

Check that the wheels are running 'true'. Spin each wheel in turn and watch where it passes a suspension arm or mudguard stay. If the wheel is buckled this will show up.

Check spoked wheels for loose or broken spokes, and all wheels for cracks or visible damage.

Regularly check wheel nuts and bolts for tightness.

Have your wheels balanced by an authorised dealer or tyre fitter.

Wheel alignment - It is important for the rear wheel to be aligned precisely behind the front. When adjusting the drive chain or refitting the rear wheel it is possible to disturb the wheel alignment. Incorrectly aligned wheels can cause

- instability, especially when cornering
- increased tyre wear.

Many motorcycles have wheel alignment guides stamped onto the frame by the chain adjusters. See your owner's manual for details.

Use the wheel alignment marks to make sure the front and rear wheels are correctly aligned

Tyres

Incorrectly inflated tyres can cause

- loss of stability
- reduced grip
- increased tyre wear.

Check your tyre pressure

- weekly
- when the tyres are cold.

The correct tyre pressure settings can be found in the owner's manual.

You might have to increase the tyre pressure

- when carrying a pillion passenger
- when carrying loads
- when riding at sustained high speeds.

In addition, check your tyres for

- tread depth and uneven tread wear
- cuts or splits
- small stones, glass or any other object stuck in the tyre
- grease or oil which could affect the tyre's grip.

If there's any sign that the tyres have been damaged they should be replaced.

Regulations - You must not use any tyre that has

- a cut longer than 25 mm or 10 per cent of the width of the tyre, whichever is the greater, and which is deep enough to reach the ply
- a lump, bulge or tear caused by the part failure of its structure
- any exposed ply or cord
- been recut.

Minimum tread - The grooves on the tread pattern of all tyres must not be less than 1 mm deep, forming a continuous band at least three quarters of the breadth of the tread and all the way around.

The groove of the original tread must be visible all around the tyre.

Most tyres have tread wear indicators. These are small raised mouldings in the bottom of the tread grooves. These indicators are exposed when the tread is worn down to 1 mm. Some tyre manufacturers design the tyres so that wear indicators are exposed before the 1 mm minimum is reached. If you can see the wear indicators use a tread depth gauge to check how much tread remains.

If you are replacing a rear tyre, make sure the new tyre is compatible with the one fitted to the front wheel

Motorcycles less than 50 cc - If your motorcycle has an engine capacity of less than 50 cc the tread of the tyre may be less than 1 mm if the base of any groove which showed in the original tread can be seen clearly.

Punctures - If your machine suddenly becomes unstable a puncture might be the cause. If this happens or a tyre bursts

- don't brake suddenly
- hold the handlebars firmly
- close the throttle to make the machine slow down
- try to keep a straight course
- stop gradually at the side of the road.

A punctured tyre should be properly repaired or replaced.

Replacing a tyre - When replacing a tyre you should

- fit a tyre that is recommended by the manufacturer
- buy the correct type. Some machines require a different type of tyre on the front and back wheel
- make sure the tyre is fitted to rotate in the direction of the tyre rotation indicators.

Controls

Brakes

There are two types of braking system fitted to motorcycles; mechanically operated and hydraulically operated. With use, various parts of the braking system will wear and need adjustment or replacement.

Mechanically operated - If your motorcycle has mechanically operated brake systems

- periodic adjustment is necessary to compensate for the strain on brake cables causing them to stretch and the wear of the brake pads or shoes
- keep the pivots and cables lubricated to maintain efficiency.

Hydraulically operated - If your motorcycle has hydraulic brakes, check

- brake fluid levels regularly
- couplings and joints for leaks
- flexible hoses for cuts or damage.

All braking systems - Brake pads and shoes gradually wear during use. Check and replace them as necessary.

If your front brakes are badly worn they will become inefficient and you could damage the brake discs

Clutch

The clutch fitted may be

- cable operated
- hydraulically operated.

If your motorcycle has a cable operated clutch check

- free play on the lever is as specified in the owner's manual
- for fraying or chafing of the cable.

For motorcycles fitted with a hydraulically operated clutch you should check for

- fluid level
- couplings and joints for leaks
- flexible hoses for cuts or damage.

Throttle

The throttle may be a single or twin cable arrangement. Check the throttle

- for smooth operation
- that it closes fully when released.

Check the cable

- for fraying or chafing
- is not pulled when turning the steering from lock to lock.

Electrical systems

Battery

Some modern batteries are maintenance-free and sealed for life. The terminals should be secure, clean and greased.

When the battery is fitted with a filler cap or caps, check the level of the fluid. The plates in each cell should be covered. Top up with distilled water if necessary, but avoid overfilling.

Lights

Check the operation of the brake lights, front and rear lights, including indicators and hazard lights if fitted, each time you use the vehicle. It's a good idea to carry a selection of spare bulbs and fuses. See your the owner's handbook for bulb/fuse replacement procedure.

Headlights must be properly adjusted to

- avoid dazzling other road users
- enable you to see the road ahead adequately.

All lights must be clean and in good working order and show a steady light.

The horn

Check the horn is working properly and sounding clearly. Take care not to alarm or annoy others when doing so.

Indicators

If fitted they must be clearly visible and in good working order. They must also flash between one and two times per second.

section **sixteen**
ACCIDENTS AND EMERGENCIES

This section covers

- o At the scene of an accident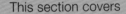
- o First aid on the road
- o Other situations

At the scene of an accident

If you're the first or among the first to arrive at the scene of an accident, remember

- further collisions can, and do, happen
- fire is a major hazard
- both the accident victims and helpers are in danger.

Warn other traffic

Do this by

- switching on hazard warning lights (if fitted) or other lights
- displaying an advance warning triangle
- using any other means to warn other drivers.

Switch off your engine and warn others to do the same. Put out cigarettes or other fire hazards and call the emergency services if necessary.

Calling emergency services - Give full details of the location and casualties. On a motorway, this could mean going to the next emergency telephone.

Mobile phones - It can be very tempting to reach immediately for your mobile phone to call the emergency services.

Before you do, make sure you are able to tell them exactly where you are. This is particularly important on a motorway where imprecise details can cause great problems for the emergency services. Location details are given on marker posts located on the hard shoulder. Always check these before you make your call.

Dealing with those involved - Move uninjured people away from the vehicles involved to a place of safety.

On a motorway, this should be away from the carriageway, hard shoulder or central reservation.

Don't move casualties trapped in vehicles unless they're in danger. Be prepared to give first aid as described later in this section.

Don't remove a motorcyclist's helmet unless it is essential to do so.

When an ambulance arrives, give the crew as many facts as you can (but not assumptions, diagnoses, etc).

Dangerous goods

If the accident involves a vehicle containing dangerous goods

- switch off your engine and do not smoke
- keep well away from the vehicle
- call the emergency services and give the police or fire brigade as much information as possible about the labels and other markings. Do not use a mobile phone close to a vehicle carrying flammable loads
- beware of dangerous liquids, dust or vapours, no matter how small a concentration, or however minor the effects on you may seem.

Full details of hazard warning plates are given in *The Highway Code*.

Passing the scene of an accident

If you are not one of the first to arrive at the scene of an accident and enough people have already stopped to give assistance, you should continue past carefully and not be distracted by the accident.

If the accident is on the other side of a dual carriageway or motorway, don't slow down to look. You may cause another accident on your side of the road, or, at the very least, additional and unnecessary traffic congestion.

Always give way to emergency vehicles. Watch out for their blue flashing lights and listen for their warning sirens.

If you are involved in an accident

You must stop.

If there are injuries, ask someone to call an ambulance and the police

Give whatever help you can. People who seem to be unhurt may be suffering from shock, and may in fact be unaware of their injuries.

Ask yourself if you're hurt too. If in doubt, get a check-up at the hospital.

You must call the police

- if anyone's hurt
- if you've damaged someone else's property but can't find them to tell them.

Report the accident, in person, to the police as soon as possible, or in any case within 24 hours.

Witnesses - Note any witnesses and try to make sure they don't leave before you get their names and addresses.

Make a note of the numbers of any vehicles whose occupants might have witnessed the accident.

You'll need to exchange details and obtain

- other people's name, address and phone numbers
- the make and registration number(s) of the other vehicle(s) involved
- insurance details.

Find out vehicle owner's details too, if different.

Information - Gather as much information as you can, such as

- damage and/or injuries caused
- weather conditions
- road conditions
- details of other vehicles. Record all information - the colour, condition, whether the lights were on, were they showing any indicator signals?
- what was said by you and other people
- identification numbers of police involved.

Take photographs - If you have a camera it can be useful to take photographs at the scene.

After an accident you will need to exchange details with other drivers involved

Draw a map - Show the situation before and after the accident, and give the distances

- between vehicles
- from road signs or junctions
- away from the kerb.

Note skid marks, where any witnesses were situated, street names and vehicle speeds and directions.

Statements - If the police ask you for a statement, you don't have to make one straight away. It could be better to wait a while, even if you don't appear to be suffering from shock.

Write your statement later. Take care with the wording, and keep a copy.

First aid on the road

The following information may be of general assistance, but there's no substitute for proper training.

Any first aid given at the scene of an accident should only be looked on as a temporary measure until the emergency services arrive.

If you haven't any first aid training the following points could be helpful.

Accident victims (adults and children)

It is essential that the following are given immediate priority if the casualty is unconscious and permanent injury is to be avoided.

Remember the letters DR A B C

D – Danger - check that you are not in danger

R – Response - try to get a response by asking questions and gently shaking their shoulder

A – Airway - the airway must be clear and kept open

B – Breathing - normal breathing must be established. If normal breathing is absent:

C – Compressions - compressions should be administered to maintain circulation (see below).

Airway: Place one hand on the forehead and two fingers under the chin and gently tilt the head back.

Breathing: Once the airway is open check breathing by placing your cheek over their mouth and nose, listen for breath, look to see if the chest rises and feel for breath, do this for up to 10 seconds.

Compressions: If they are not breathing normally place two hands in the centre of the chest and press down 4-5cms at a rate of 100/minute. You may only need one hand for a child. Give 30 chest compressions.

Then tilt the head back gently, pinch the casualty's nostrils together and place your mouth over theirs. Give two breaths, each lasting one second (use gentle breaths for a small child).

Continue with cycles of 30 chest compressions and 2 breaths until medical help arrives.

Accident victims (infants, under 1 year)

Use the same procedures as for the adults and children, except

- Use two fingers in the middle of the chest when delivering compressions
- To deliver breaths make a seal over the infant's mouth AND nose with your mouth.

Unconscious and breathing

Do not move a casualty unless there's further danger. Movement could add to spinal/neck injury.

If breathing is not normal or stops, treat as recommended in the breathing section.

Don't attempt to remove a motorcyclist's helmet unless it's essential – (casualty not breathing normally), otherwise serious injury could result.

If an adult or child is unconscious and breathing, place them on their side in the recovery position (as shown below).

- Place the arm nearest you in a right angle, move the other arm, palm upwards, against the casualty's cheek.

- With your other hand grasp the far leg, just above the knee and pull it up, keeping the foot flat on the ground.

- Pull the knee towards you, keeping their hand pressed against their cheek and position the leg at a right angle.

Make sure their airway remains open and that you monitor the casualty's condition until medical help arrives.

Bleeding

First check for anything that may be in the wound, such as glass. Taking care not to press on the object, build up padding on either side of the object. If there is nothing embedded, apply firm pressure over the wound to stem the flow of blood. As soon as practical, fasten a pad to the wound with a bandage or length of cloth. Use the cleanest material available.

If a limb is bleeding but not broken, raise it above the level of the heart to reduce the flow of blood. Any restriction of blood circulation for more than a short time could cause long-term injuries. It is vital to obtain skilled medical help as soon as possible. Make sure that someone dials 999 or 112.

Dealing with shock

The effects of shock may not be immediately obvious. Warning signs to look for include

- rapid pulse
- pale grey skin
- sweating
- rapid shallow breathing.

Prompt treatment can help to deal with shock

- don't give the casualty anything to eat or drink
- reassure the victim confidently and keep checking on them
- keep casualties warm and make them as comfortable as you can
- talk firmly and quietly to anyone who's hysterical
- don't let shock victims wander into the path of other traffic
- try not to leave any casualty alone
- don't move the casualty unless it's necessary
- if a casualty does need to be moved for their own safety, take care to avoid making their injuries worse.

Burns

Check the casualty for shock, and if possible, try to cool the burn for at least 10 minutes. Try to find a liquid that is clean, cold and non-toxic with which to douse it.

Do not try to remove anything that is sticking to the burn.

Be prepared

Always carry a first aid kit - you might never need it, but it could save a life.

Learn First Aid - you can learn first aid from a qualified organisation such as

- St Johns Ambulance and Brigade
- St Andrew's Ambulance Association
- British Red Cross Society

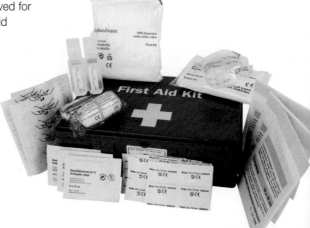

Other situations

Tunnels

If you break down or have an accident in a tunnel

- switch on your hazard warning lights (if fitted) and switch off the engine
- call for help from the nearest emergency point
- give first aid to any injured people, if you are able.

If your vehicle is on fire

- pull over to the side, switch off the engine and put the machine on its stand
- attempt to put out the fire using either an extinguisher carried on your motorcycle or the one available in the tunnel
- call for help from the nearest emergency point
- move without delay to an emergency exit if you cannot put out the fire.

If the vehicle in front is on fire switch on your warning lights, then follow the above procedure, giving first aid to the injured if possible.

Fire

Carrying a suitable fire extinguisher on your motorcycle may help you to put out a small fire. Although, even a small fire can spread with alarming speed and any fire should be treated with extreme caution.

If the fire appears to be large do not try to tackle it; get well clear of the vehicle and leave it to the fire brigade. Do not take any risks.

When using your motorcycle, if you notice a strong smell of petrol, don't ignore it – investigate!

In most tunnels emergency exits will be shown by an illuminated sign

Fire extinguishers don't take up a lot of space and could save a small fire from becoming a serious incident

section **seventeen**
ENVIRONMENTAL RIDING

This section covers

- Eco-safe driving
- Vehicle maintenance

Eco-safe riding

Transport is an essential part of modern life, but we cannot ignore its environmental consequences – local, regional and global. There's increasing public concern for the protection of our environment, with the result that many car and motorcycle manufacturers are devoting more time, effort and resources to the development of environmentally-friendly vehicles and machines.

If you follow the principles of Eco-safe riding, set out in the following pages you will become a more environmentally-friendly rider – your journeys will be more comfortable and you could considerably reduce your fuel bills and reduce those emissions that cause damage to the atmosphere.

But more importantly you will become a safer rider, as you develop your planning, perception and anticipation skills to a high level.

Although it is good to save fuel you must not compromise the safety of yourself and other road users when attempting to do so. Road Safety is more important than fuel saving. At all times you should be prepared to adapt to changing conditions and it may be that you have to sacrifice fuel saving for safety.

Air pollution

Air pollution contributes to health problems for many people. Road transport accounts for around 20% of all emissions and in densely populated areas traffic is the biggest source of air pollution.

The particular problem with emissions from motor vehicles (including motorcycles) is that they are at ground level and people with conditions like respiratory problems, heart or vascular disease, are particularly exposed. Motor vehicles account for most of the movement of people and goods. In addition, pollution also causes changes to communities and the landscape including

- damage to vegetation
- deterioration and weakening of buildings and bridges
- the depletion of natural resources
- disruption of wildlife.

Fuel combustion produces carbon dioxide and nitric oxides, both major greenhouse gases, and transport accounts for about one-fifth of the carbon dioxide we produce in this country. Catalytic converters in good working order reduce these emissions.

Information about air pollution is available on

- Ceefax or Teletext
- Air Pollution Information Service - Freephone 0800 556677
- local radio or newspapers
- the internet at www.defra.gov.uk/environment

Everyone has a responsibility to do what they can to safeguard the environment for future generations

What you can do to help

Using motor vehicles has become a central feature in our lives, but it is still possible to use them in a manner more beneficial to the environment by taking a little care and thought. We give some suggestions about what you can do to help on the following pages.

Become an eco-safe rider

Eco-safe riding is a style of riding that contributes to road safety whilst reducing fuel consumption and emissions.

One of the main factors in increasing road safety is the emphasis on planning ahead so that you are prepared in advance for potential hazards. Making this a feature of your riding will also mean you use less fuel.

Forward planning - While riding you should be constantly scanning all around. Check into the far distance, midground and foreground, also check behind and to the sides by frequent use of all your mirrors. When following another vehicle keeping a safe distance from it will help you to see further ahead.

Early recognition of potential hazards is important, but just looking isn't enough. You need to act correctly on what you have seen and this will mean you're able to anticipate problems and take appropriate action in good time.

Early action should ensure you're travelling at the correct speed when dealing with a hazard and this avoids the need for late braking or harsh acceleration, both of which lead to higher fuel consumption.

If you plan early for hazards you will also avoid causing bunching of other road users, traffic will flow more smoothly and you will use less fuel.

Starting up - If your motorcycle is fitted with a choke and you need to use it to start the engine when it's cold, move the choke control to off as soon as the engine will run smoothly without it.

Riding away - Avoid over-revving your engine when you start your machine and try to pull away smoothly.

Choosing your speed

Always ride within the speed limit. Exceeding a speed limit by only a few miles per hour will mean that you use more fuel but, more importantly, you are breaking the law and increasing the risk of serious injury if you're involved in a collision.

Slow down. Motor vehicles travelling at 70mph use up to 30% more fuel to cover the same distance as those travelling at 50mph. However don't travel so slowly that you inconvenience other road users.

The throttle - Try to use the throttle smoothly and progressively. Avoid rapid acceleration or heavy braking as this leads to greater fuel consumption and more pollution. Riding smoothly can reduce fuel consumption by about 15% as well as reducing wear and tear on your machine.

Selecting gears - As soon as conditions allow, use the highest gear possible without making the engine struggle.

Check your fuel consumption

Check your fuel consumption regularly. To make sure you are getting the most from your machine, simply record the amount of fuel you put in against miles travelled. This will help you to check whether you're using fuel efficiently.

An increase in the average fuel consumption can mean you need to have your motorcycle serviced.

An eco-friendly rider is constantly aware of how much fuel their machine uses.

Using a trip computer can help you check your fuel consumption.

Route planning

Avoid making unnecessary short journeys.

Plan your route and avoid known hold ups and road works. Always know where you're going - you'll use a lot of fuel by getting lost.

Plan your journey beforehand and try to use uncongested routes. Continuous research has resulted in new methods of helping the environment by easing traffic flow.

If you're likely to be making a prolonged stop, say for more than two minutes at a level crossing or road works, you may consider it best to stop the engine.

Off-road activities

If you take part in off-road activities, remember

- avoid damaging fences, paths, grassland etc
- take care not to harm livestock or wildlife
- respect the countryside in general
- ride in a responsible manner at all times

Machine maintenance

You should make sure that your machine is serviced and maintained regularly.

- Make sure the engine is tuned correctly. Badly-tuned engines use more fuel and emit more exhaust fumes.

- Have your machine serviced as recommended by the manufacturer. The cost of a service may well be less than the cost of running it in a badly-maintained state. For example, even slight brake drag can increase the fuel consumption.

- Make sure your garage includes an emissions check in the service.

- Make sure that your tyres are properly inflated. Incorrect tyre pressure results in shorter tyre life and may create a danger as it can affect stability and braking capacity. In addition, under inflation can increase fuel consumption and emissions.

- If you do your own motorcycle maintenance, make sure that you send oil, old batteries and used tyres to a garage or local authority site for recycling or safe disposal. Don't pour oil down the drain. It's illegal, harmful to the environment and could lead to prosecution.

- Use good quality engine oil - if you use synthetic engine oils rather than the cheaper mineral oil, you can save fuel.

Routine servicing ensures your engine is running at its most efficient and this keeps exhaust emissions to a minimum

245

section **eighteen**
TRAFFIC CONGESTION

This section covers
o Avoiding congestion
o Schemes to deal with congestion

Avoiding congestion

Journey planning

Time of day - If possible try to plan your journey so as to avoid the busy times of day. Congestion is often caused by work/school related travel and this causes delays in the early morning and late afternoon/early evening. Try to avoid these times, this will

- allow you to have an easier and more pleasant journey and one that is less likely to experience delays
- ease the congestion caused by work/school traffic.

Try to arrange appointments so that you avoid these times.

Plan your route - Make sure you know where you're going by planning your route beforehand. If possible plan alternatives in case you find your original route blocked, especially if you are travelling alone on an unknown route.

Before travelling, plan your route.

- Look at a map.
- Consult a motoring organisation or a route planner available on the internet.
- Print out or write down your route.

Your journey

Leave plenty of time for your journey. Concern about reaching your destination in time can lead to frustration and the increased tendency to take risks which could lead to an accident.

Carry a map with you so that you can check your position or identify an alternative route if you get held up or diverted.

Consider fitting a Global Positioning System (GPS) on your motorcycle as this will identify your route for you.

Mobile phones - A mobile phone can be useful in case of delays or breakdowns, but remember that it is illegal to use one while riding, and that includes while you are waiting in a queue of traffic.

Hazard Perception - Slow down early - if you do this the traffic situation in front will often have cleared by the time you get there.

Constant speed - When you can see well ahead and the road conditions are good, you should drive at a steady speed. Choose a speed that is within the speed limit and one that you and your motorcycle can handle safely.

At busy times there are some stretches of motorway which have variable speed limits shown on the gantries above the lanes. The maximum speed limits shown on these signals are mandatory.

These speed limits are in place to make traffic proceed at a constant speed as this has been shown to reduce bunching. By keeping traffic at a constant speed over a longer distance, congestion has been shown to ease.

Your overall journey time normally improves by keeping to the constant speed, even if at times it may appear that you could have travelled faster for shorter periods.

Looking well ahead to see what the traffic in front of you is doing will enable you to plan ahead

Lane discipline - Follow the normal rules relating to lane discipline (see pages 118 and 177) to avoid holding up traffic behind you.

On motorways, you must not normally ride on the hard shoulder, but at road works and certain places where signs direct, the hard shoulder may become the left lane.

Using sign information - Look well ahead for signals or signs, especially on a motorway.

On very busy stretches, there may be overhead gantries with messages about congestion ahead and a separate signal for each lane. The messages may also give an alternative route which you should use if at all possible.

If you're not sure whether to use the alternative route, take the next exit, pull over at the first available safe area (lay by or service area) and look at a map.

Remember, on a motorway, once you have passed an exit and encounter congestion, there may not be another opportunity to leave and you could be stuck in slow-moving or stationary traffic for some time. Take the opportunity when it arises, you can always rejoin the motorway if you feel that is the best course of action once you have had time to consider the options.

Motorway signals can be used to warn you of a danger ahead. For example, there may be an accident, fog, or a spillage, which you may not immediately be able to see (see page 174).

249

Schemes to deal with congestion

Active Traffic Management

Active Traffic Management (ATM) is a new pilot project to try to reduce congestion and make journey times more reliable. It will be carried out on the M42 in the West Midlands.

ATM will feature benefits including

- monitoring by close circuit television
- high-visibility driver information panels
- new lighting
- new emergency roadside telephones
- Emergency Refuge Areas for vehicles to use in an emergency or breakdown

- use of the hard-shoulder as an additional running lane under controlled conditions to manage traffic in peak congestion or during an incident
- Highways Agency Traffic Officer patrols monitoring the motorway.

Emergency Refuge Areas - These are 100 metres long, wider than the hard-shoulder and are located about every 500 metres. Features include

- sensors to alert the control centre that a vehicle has entered
- CCTV enabling the control centre to monitor the vehicles and send assistance

---

Active traffic management signals

 A speed limit shown in a red ring gives a mandatory speed limit for traffic travelling in the lane over which it is shown.

 A red cross above the hard shoulder means you should not use this lane except in an emergency or breakdown. It will not be accompanied by flashing beacons.

Gantries are used to display information and are about 500 metres apart.

- new generation Emergency Roadside Telephones containing additional multilingual and hard of hearing support
- additional distance from the main carriageway.

Riding in actively managed areas - As with any motorway, you must obey the signals displayed on the overhead gantries.

There are three driving scenarios

- normal motorway driving conditions
- actively managed mode
- hard-shoulder running mode.

Normal Motorway Conditions

- No congestion or incident.
- No speed limits shown on signals.
- National speed limits apply.
- Hard shoulder for emergency & breakdown use only.

Actively Managed Mode

- There may be an incident or congestion ahead.
- All speed limit signals are set and must be obeyed.
- Driver information panels will provide information for road users.
- Red cross over hard shoulder means do not use this lane, except in an emergency or breakdown (the red cross will not be accompanied by flashing beacons).

Hard Shoulder Running Mode - This is similar to the actively managed mode, except that the hard shoulder may be used as a running lane between junctions. In this case the red cross above the hard shoulder will be replaced by the appropriate speed limit.

Highways Agency Traffic Officers

Working in partnership with the police, Highways Agency Traffic Officers are a new highly-trained and highly-visible service patrolling the motorway to help keep traffic moving and make your journey as safe and reliable as possible.

Traffic Officers wear a high-visibility orange and yellow jacket, and drive a high visibility vehicle with yellow and black chequered markings. They will have a unique identification number and photographic identity card.

Role of a traffic officer - They will

- help broken-down motorists
- offer safety advice to motorists
- clear debris from the carriageway
- undertake high-visibility patrols
- support the police and emergency services during incidents
- provide mobile/temporary road closures and manage diversion routes.

If you have an emergency or breakdown on the motorway the best action to take is to use an emergency roadside telephone.

Emergency roadside telephones are answered by Highways Agency control centre operators located in a regional control centre. Control centre operators are able to monitor any stranded motorists on close circuit television screens and despatch the nearest available traffic officer patrol to assist.

Powers of traffic officers - Unlike the police, traffic officers will not have any enforcement powers, however they are able to stop and direct anyone travelling on the motorway. It is an offence not to comply with the directions given by a traffic officer.

Extent of scheme - Seven regional control centres, managed by the Highways Agency, are able to despatch traffic officers to any motorway in England.

Urban Congestion Schemes

Congestion in urban areas leads to

- longer journey times
- frustration
- pollution through standing and slow-moving traffic.

London suffers the worst traffic congestion in the UK and amongst the worst in Europe. Various measures have been introduced to try to reduce and alleviate the congestion and make traffic flow more freely. 'Red Routes' and 'Congestion charging' are two of the schemes initiated in the London area. These may be introduced into other congested towns and cities.

Red Routes - These keep traffic moving and reduce the pollution that comes from vehicle emissions. Stopping and parking is allowed only within marked boxes.

There are five main types of Red Route markings.

- Double red lines - stopping is not allowed at any time, for any reason.

- Single red lines - parking, loading or picking up passengers is not allowed during the day (generally 7am to 7pm). Stopping is allowed outside these hours and on Sunday.

- Red boxes - indicate parking or loading is permitted during the day at off-peak times, normally 10am to 4pm. Some allow loading and some allow parking, the rules in each case are clearly shown on a sign beside the box.

- White boxes - indicate that parking or loading may be allowed at any time, restrictions being clearly shown on the sign beside the box.

- Red route clearway - there are no road markings but clearway signs indicate that stopping isn't allowed at any time apart from in marked lay-bys.

Congestion charging - Motorcycles are currently exempt from congestion charging.

section **nineteen**
EUROPEAN TRAVEL

This section covers
- Travelling in europe
- Planning your journey
- Your motorcycle
- Motorcycle documents
- Personal documents
- Motoring regulations
- Riding in europe

Travelling in Europe

Taking your motorcycle abroad, or hiring one in the country you're visiting, gives you freedom and mobility.

You can

- plan your holiday around your interests or business commitments
- travel at your own pace
- stop when and where you like
- visit places of interest on the way
- discover the more remote places
- carry equipment such as camping gear.

This section summarises what you need to do to prepare for riding in Europe.

An extensive motorway network runs through most of Europe and there are regular ferry links from many UK ports.

> **Remember,** many East European countries have now opened up their borders, so there's even more of Europe to explore.

You have more opportunity to choose routes which take you closer to your European destination.

The Channel Tunnel provides yet another link to continental Europe.

You will find you need to concentrate fully when you begin to ride on the right and this can soon become tiring

Planning your journey

If you're planning to take your motorcycle abroad, the major motoring organisations can help you to organise and plan the details of your trip. They can

- save you time and money
- set up medical, travel and machine insurance
- provide equipment for minor repairs and breakdowns
- help you organise the correct documents for your motorcycle or trailer.

You can often make your trip much easier by using their facilities and experience.

Your route

Once you know which country you're going to visit, you can begin to plan your route.

Again, the motoring organisations can simplify this for you with

- computerised route guides
- summaries of motoring regulations
- details of tolls, etc.

They will recommend routes from continental ports or airports to specific destinations, using motorways for speed and convenience, or scenic routes for pleasure.

When planning a trip abroad pay attention to all the details, you don't want to find you have forgotten something once you have left the UK

Your motorcycle

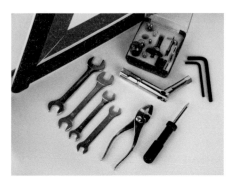

Carrying spare bulbs and fuses in your toolkit should prevent minor problems spoiling your trip

Precautions against breakdown

Dealing with breakdowns abroad can be especially time consuming and worrying without the help of one of the motoring organisations or breakdown services.

The best prevention is to have your motorcycle thoroughly serviced before you leave and to make regular checks on route.

You can also make sure you're prepared for minor breakdowns.

Checks to make include

- spare bulbs and fuses
- your toolkit; make sure all items are complete and in working order
- make sure you have a spare key.

Lights

Your lights will need to be altered for riding on the right.

- Deflectors are required in most countries. These prevent your dipped beam dazzling drivers approaching on the left
- Yellow-tinted headlights are no longer required in most countries
- Carry a set of replacement bulbs and fuses.

Emergency equipment

In many countries emergency equipment must be carried. Check with motoring organisations to find out what is required in the countries you will be visiting. This equipment may include

- emergency repair kits
- spares kit
- emergency warning triangle.

257

Motorcycle documents

You must have all the necessary documents before leaving. Again, the motoring organisations will be able to tell you what's required for each country.

Insurance

Third party motor vehicle insurance is compulsory in most countries. It is strongly recommended you contact your insurer to make sure you're adequately covered.

Most insurance policies issued in the UK automatically provide third party cover in EC countries as well as in some others. They do not provide comprehensive cover unless you arrange this with your insurer, who may charge an extra premium. Make sure you have the appropriate insurance certificate with you. Certain countries require a bail bond as a security in the event of an accident. Consult your insurer.

Your driving licence

You must carry your national driving licence when motoring abroad. Even if you need an International Driving Permit (see below), take your national licence also.

If you want to ride a hired or borrowed motorcycle in the country you're visiting, ask about minimum age requirements in case they apply to you.

In Italy, you must carry either a translation with your licence or an International Driving Permit. If you have a pink or pink and green EC-type UK licence, this translation isn't required.

International Driving Permit

Many non-EC countries still require an International Driving Permit (IDP).

To qualify for one, you must be 18 or over. To apply you'll need

- your driving licence
- a passport-sized photograph
- a fee.

The motoring organisations can issue your IDP.

Vehicle Registration Certificate

You must carry the original Vehicle Registration Certificate with you.

If you don't have your Vehicle Registration Certificate, apply to a Vehicle Registration Office for a temporary certificate of registration (V379). Apply through your local Post Office well in advance of your journey.

If you plan to hire, borrow or lease a vehicle, you must ensure you have all the relevant documents.

Personal documents

Passport/visa

All persons travelling must either hold, or be named on, an up-to-date passport valid for all countries through which you intend to travel.

Carry your passport(s) at all times.

Keep a separate note of the number, date and place of issue of each passport, in case they are stolen or lost.

Travellers need a visa for some European countries. Check well in advance with the embassies or consulates concerned. This is particularly important if you hold a UK passport not issued in this country, or the passport of any other country.

Medical expenses insurance

You're strongly advised to take out comprehensive medical insurance cover for any trip abroad.

Most medical treatment can be obtained free of charge or at reduced cost from the healthcare schemes of countries with whom the UK has reciprocal healthcare arrangements.

However, don't rely on these arrangements alone.

Department of Health leaflet E111 is available from any Post Office. It provides health advice for travellers.

Take great care of your passport and keep a note of who to contact in case it is lost or stolen

Motoring regulations

Drink and riding

Don't drink and ride. The laws and penalties abroad are often more severe than those in the UK.

Advance warning triangle

The use of a warning triangle is compulsory in most countries for all vehicles with more than two wheels (including side-car outfits). Hazard warning lights should not be used instead of a triangle, but to complement it. Some countries require two advance warning triangles.

Spare bulbs

Some countries require you to carry a spare set of bulbs.

First aid kit

Make sure your vehicle carries a first aid kit. It is compulsory in some countries and strongly recommended in many others.

Identification plate

If you're towing a trailer, fit an identification plate.

Nationality plate

You must display a nationality plate of the approved size and design at the rear of your motorcycle or trailer.

Speed limits

There are speed limits in all countries, but they vary from country to country.

A list of the speed limits can be obtained from the motoring organisations. Make sure you know the limits for those countries you will be travelling through.

Obey all speed limits. Many countries have severe on-the-spot fines for offenders. Others prosecute, and that could prove to be expensive.

Warning: police fines - On-the-spot fines are imposed for most minor motoring offences. Make sure you know the regulations for each country you intend visiting and obey them.

Riding in Europe

It can take you time to adjust to riding on the right. Mistakes can lead to accidents.

When taking rear observation remember you're now riding on the right. This is particularly important before deciding to overtake. Rear observation to the left is vitally important.

Make certain you feel fit enough for your trip. Don't let your attention wander. It can be dangerous to forget where you are, even for a moment.

Each time you set out, remember that you're in a foreign country where you must ride on the right.

Avoid riding for long periods and don't allow fatigue to set in.

> **Remember,** hire motorcycles may be unfamiliar. Make sure you understand the controls layout before you ride.

Take special care after a rest when you return onto the road again.

Defensive riding

Take extra care at roundabouts. Be aware of the changed priority. Don't attempt to overtake until you're used to riding on the right.

Motorway tolls

Some countries charge motorway tolls. Find out about these and include them in your budget.

Security

Loss of possessions, passports, tickets, cash and credit cards can be distressing and inconvenient when you're abroad.

Be on your guard against confidence tricksters.

Checklist

As part of your planning, make a checklist of equipment, documents and other items.

If you're travelling through several countries, check against each item whether it's compulsory or strongly recommended.

After your trip

Don't forget to adjust to riding on the left again as soon as you return!

Index

The OFFICIAL DSA GUIDE to
RIDING
the essential skills

WIN OFFICIAL SUZUKI GEAR*

TSO, DSA's official publishing partner, is offering you the chance to win new Suzuki clothing or accessories.

Please send the entry form to:
Win Bike Gear Competition, TSO, Freepost, ANG 4748, Norwich, NR3 1YX

Competition Rules

1 Only one entry accepted per purchase.

2 All entries must be on official entry forms. No photocopies will be accepted.

3 Entries must be received by 8 September 2008.

4 The competition will run from 23 July 2007 to 8 September 2008 and one prize shall be awarded. All entries must be received by 8 September 2008. No responsibility can be taken by the Promoter for lost, late, misdirected or stolen entries.

5 The prize will be a set of genuine Suzuki leathers or protective clothing, gloves, helmet and accessories to be selected by Suzuki at a value of about £1000 at time of going to press in its absolute discretion. Colour is subject to availability. The size of bike gear will be based on measurements supplied by the winner and accessories will be based on the type of bike to be used by the winner, upon request by Suzuki, failing which Suzuki shall be entitled to select reasonable sizes and accessories for the winner. There will be no cash alternatives.

6 Only entrants over the age of 16 and resident in the UK are eligible.

7 The winning entry will be decided on 10 September 2008 from all correct entries received by the closing date. The winner will be notified by 24 September 2008. Only the winner will be contacted personally.

8 The winner will be contacted via the email address or telephone number they provide. The Promoter will not be held responsible if the winner cannot be contacted by the means they gave.

9 The winner's name will be published on the Promoter's website at www.tso.co.uk.

10 The prize will be made available within six weeks of the closing date.

11 By accepting any Prize, entrants consent to the use for promotional and other purposes (without further payment and except as prohibited by law) of their name, address, likeness and Prize information. The winner may be required to participate in the Promoter's reasonable marketing and promotional activities. By entering into this competition you consent to participate in the Promoter's reasonable marketing and promotional activities. The winning entrant agrees that all rights including copyright in all works created by the entrant as part of the competition entry shall be owned by the Promoter absolutely without the need for further payment being made to the entrant. Such entrant further agrees to waive unconditionally and irrevocably all moral rights pursuant to the Copyright, Designs and Patents Act of 1988 and under any similar law in force from time to time anywhere in the world in respect of all such works.

12 The Promoter reserves the right to cancel this competition at any stage, if deemed necessary in its opinion, and if circumstances arise outside of its control.

13 Entrants will be deemed to have accepted these rules and to agree to be bound by them when entering this competition.

14 This competition is not open to employees or contractors of the Promoter or the Driving Standards Agency or any person directly involved in the organisation or running of the competition, or their direct family members. The judge's decision is final in every situation including any not covered above and no correspondence will be entered into.

15 The Promoter is The Stationery Office Limited, St Crispins, Duke Street, Norwich, NR3 1PD (the publishers of The Official DSA Learner Range).